Design of an Interactive
Manipulator Programming Environment

Computer Science:
Artificial Intelligence, No. 16

Harold S. Stone, Ph.D., Series Editor

IBM Corporation
T.J. Watson Research Center
Yorktown, New York

Other Titles in This Series

Design of an Interactive
Manipulator Programming Environment

by
Ron Goldman

UMI RESEARCH PRESS
Ann Arbor, Michigan

Produced and distributed by
UMI Research Press
an imprint of
University Microfilms International
A Xerox Information Resources Company
Ann Arbor, Michigan 48106

Library of Congress Cataloging in Publication Data

Goldman, Ron, 1952-
Design of an interactive manipulator programming
environment.

(Computer science. Artificial intelligence ;
no. 16)
Originally presented as the author's Ph.D. thesis
(Stanford, 1983)
Bibliography: p.
Includes index.
1. Robots—Programming. 2. AL (Computer program
language) I. Title. II. Title: Interactive
manipulator programming. III. Series.
TJ211.G65 1985 629.8'92 84-28091
ISBN 0-8357-1616-3 (alk. paper)

To the Muse of Music

Contents

List of Figures

Acknowledgments

I would like to thank all of those friends and colleagues who helped in making this book a reality. This includes Tom Binford, John Hennessey and John McCarthy for reading the manuscript; Dick Gabriel for his helpful comments and proofreading of the initial draft; past and present members of the Stanford robotics group, in particular, John Craig, Maria and Pina Gini, Jim Maples, Shahid Mujtaba, Ken Salisbury, Bruce Shimano, and Rick Vistnes; members of the systems support staff at the Stanford AI lab, Don Coates, Marty Frost, and Ted Panofsky; Rich Pattis and Polle Zellweger for fruitful discussions about debugging; and all the others who made the Stanford AI lab such an agreeable place to work. And special thanks to Lisa Jane, Sally Ann, Angeline, Dinah, Betty Likens, Nancy Rowland, and, especially, Sally Ann Johnson.

1

Introduction

The last twenty years have seen the development of a new class of machines—robot manipulators. These mechanical arms are controlled by computers, which potentially makes them capable of a wide variety of tasks. Research done over the last two decades has attempted to achieve this potential.

Previous work has focused primarily on low-level arm servo control to increase the basic capabilities of manipulators, on design of manipulator programming languages to make it easier to express the description of a task to be done by the manipulator, and on high-level attempts to automate the writing of these programs.

Until high-level planning systems become a reality, the programming of manipulators will remain a task for human programmers. In writing manipulator programs various problems arise, some of which are identical to those faced in writing conventional computer programs, while others are unique to the manipulator domain. As the development of working manipulator programs can be a very difficult and time-consuming activity, it is important to provide tools to aid in this task.

Recent work in the area of programming environments has been directed toward creating better tools for the development of conventional computer programs. The aim of this book is to extend this work to the manipulator programming domain.

1.1 Background

Over the last decade the Stanford hand-eye group has been working in the area of manipulator languages. Early work with the WAVE language [Bolles and Paul 1973] was followed by the design and implementation of AL [Finkel et al. 1974]. AL is an ALGOL-like language extended to handle the problems of manipulator control. Basic data types include vectors, used to represent translations, velocities, and locations; frames, which represent local coordinate systems, i.e. position and orientation; and events, used to synchronize parallel processes. Appropriate arithmetic operators (e.g. cross product, transformations from one coordinate system to another, etc.) exist to handle these data types. Through the use of affixment it is possible to build up objects consisting of various features (i.e. frames) and the relationships between them. These affixment structures are then maintained as the objects are moved about. In addition to normal ALGOL control structure, AL allows statements to be executed in parallel; simple signal and wait primitives are provided for synchronization purposes. Manipulator motion is specified with the MOVE statement which allows detailed control of both the arm's trajectory and its dynamics. In addition certain conditions (forces, durations, events, etc.) may be monitored during motions, and if a given condition occurs, appropriate actions may be taken. These condition monitors are another way of achieving parallel processing in AL. A fuller description of the AL language is given in the final section of this introductory chapter.

The initial implementation of AL consisted of a compiler, running on a DEC KL10 (SAIL), and a runtime system on a PDP-11/45 to which the arms are connected. Manipulator work done in this environment revealed that much could be gained by using an interpretive system, involving the manipulator, to define the locations of objects in the manipulator's work space, and to build up the affixment structures describing them. An auxiliary system, called POINTY, was developed to provide this interactive capability. It consisted of a command interpreter on SAIL which talked to the AL runtime system on the PDP-11/45. Eventually POINTY grew to handle most types of AL statements and was used to write and test out manipulator programs. The POINTY system, however, was somewhat cumbersome to use for this due to the lack of editing features, the low bandwidth between the two machines, and the lack of debugging features in the runtime system.

The next step in developing AL was to bring up a highly interactive AL system which would allow the user either to enter single AL statements for immediate execution or to use an editor to create an AL program for future execution. Programs could be debugged and modified on-line. Special debugging features would exist including breakpoints and single-stepping; the user could freely alter control flow to try out program segments, display gathered force data, and fully access the interpreter's ability to examine and change variables, and execute AL statements. Such a system, allowing manipulator programs to be written, modified, debugged, and run in a single environment, would provide a more efficient man-machine interface between the programmer and the manipulators.

The goal of this research has been to design and implement such an interactive manipulator programming environment. The resulting system consists of an interpreter with source-level debugging facilities, a syntax-directed display editor knowledgeable about AL, and a force graphics subsystem.

1.2   Organization of the Book

The rest of this chapter briefly discusses some of the previous work that has been done in the areas of manipulator programming languages and programming environments. It concludes with a short description of the AL language.

Chapter 2 examines some of the problems relating to manipulator programming. It first describes several of the difficulties that arise from including the physical world as a part of the programming environment and the consequent problems of programming in this environment. Then some specific issues relating to manipulator programming are discussed, such as object definition, motion control, use of force and compliance, error recovery, and parallelism. Last is a discussion of the requirements for a successful manipulator programming environment in light of these problems.

Chapter 3 describes the newly designed AL manipulator programming environment from the user's viewpoint and attempts to show how it facilitates the creation, debugging and running of manipulator programs. It describes the interpreter, the syntax-directed editor, the debugging facilities, and the force graphics subsystem. Examples are given showing how the system works in actual operation.

Chapter 4 goes into some of the details of the implementation of the current AL system. It discusses the way a program is internally represented, along with the other data structures used in the system. The insides of the interpreter, the editor, debugging facilities, and the force graphics subsystem are also described.

Finally, chapter 5 provides a summary of the major points covered in the book and mentions some topics for future work.

Two appendixes are provided. The first gives a short summary of the AL language. The second lists the various commands that can be performed by the AL editor and debugging system.

1.3 Previous Work

This book is a result of extending recent work done in the area of programming environments to the problems faced in manipulator programming. This section will present a brief overview of that work. First several existing manipulator programming systems will be discussed. Then some recent work in programming environments will be described.

Manipulator Programming Systems

A manipulator programming system consists of two quite distinct parts. First is the manipulator programming language in which the user can issue commands to the manipulators. Second, and equally important, is the user interface to the system—that is, the tools provided the user in developing the program. Both aspects of several existing manipulator programming systems will be discussed below.

Spectrum of manipulator languages. Over the years a number of different manipulator languages have been developed. These languages span a wide range in the features they offer. Many are oriented towards basic research in robotics and are primarily laboratory tools, while others are aimed at actual production use. A few even claim to be both. Some are intended for experienced programmers, while others are expected to be utilized by more naive users.

Some manipulator systems have been developed by taking an existing programming language and adding special routines that the user can call to control the manipulator, for example RTL/2 (INDA [Park and Burnett 1979]). Others have chosen to create new languages with special primitives for manipulator control.

The manipulator languages that have been developed range from early designs similar to assembly-level computer languages (WAVE [Paul 1976], EMILY [Will and Grossman 1975]), to intermediate level languages ([Rosen et al. 1977], VAL [Unimation 1979], PAL [Takase, Paul, and Berg 1979]), to others based on extending higher level languages like ALGOL (AL [Goldman and Mujtaba 1981]) and PL/I (MAPLE [Darringer and Blasgen 1975]), and to newly designed high-level languages (AML [Taylor, Summers, and Myer 1982]). Some of these are general purpose programming languages, while others are quite limited. For example, some of the earlier languages cannot update a variable's value or can do so only in a very limited manner, while others can do extensive arithmetic.

The manipulator-specific extensions that have been made in designing these languages include motion control, new data types (e.g. vectors, frames), concurrency and synchronization. New language constructs are continually being added as the capabilities of computer-controlled manipulator servoing increases.

Another distinction between the various manipulator languages is the level at which the user describes the task to be performed. Early languages required all of the motions to be explicitly described in terms of the manipulator. Later languages, such as AL, allow motions to be expressed in terms of the object being moved, with the system automatically translating this into the corresponding manipulator motions. At an even higher level are the planning systems (AUTOPASS [Lieberman and Wesley 1977], LAMA [Lozano-Perez 1976], RAPT [Popplestone, Ambler, and Bellos 1978]). These are intended to take task-level descriptions of the assembly and convert them into low-level manipulator code. Planning systems require a geometric data base which models the shape of each object in the assembly. This contrasts with current manipulator systems which have minimal, if any, models of the objects.

Systems support.   Just as the expressive power of the different manipulator languages varies, so does the level of user support provided by the actual implementation. Most implementations of manipulator languages consist merely of a compiler and a simple runtime system to execute programs. These systems (AL, MAPLE, LM [Latombe and Mazer 1981]) essentially provide no support to the user who is trying to debug a manipulator program. Debugging consists of repeating the traditional edit-compile-test loop until the program works. This can be very tedious. There tends to be a long delay between writing a statement and trying it out. Also, any state associated with the program is lost when the user reloads a new version of the program.

The next level of support is provided by interpretive systems where the user can enter statements for immediate execution (WAVE, POINTY, AML, the German implementation of AL [Blume 1981], PAL). Some of these systems allow the running program to be paused, breakpoints to be set and cleared, variables to be examined and modified, and other statements to be executed while the program is suspended. Others are just simple interpreters with few, if any, of the above capabilities. One of the features of systems in this class is the ability to teach positions with the manipulator and record them in the developing program. A helpful tool to facilitate this teaching is the ability to position the manipulator through the use of joysticks, teach boxes, or voice recognition devices. None of these systems allow the running program to be modified, though some (WAVE, POINTY) have minimal editing facilities for macros which allows a sequence of statements to be tried, modified, and retried easily. The direct interaction between the user and the manipulator that this level of system supplies greatly facilitates the development of working manipulator programs.

Still better is the system where the user can actually edit the running program and exercise some control over its execution (INDA,VAL). In the case of VAL this editing can be performed while the program is running, while other systems require the program to be paused before allowing it to be edited. Unfortunately, the editing and debugging facilities currently available in these systems are quite primitive. Still, any editing ability helps the user tremendously.

Systems which provide direct assistance in writing the program have also been developed. POINTY aids the user by creating the declaration statements needed by an AL program to define the objects being worked with. XPROBE [Summers and Grossman 1981] conducts a dialog with the user who guides the manipulator through an example of the desired task. From this the XPROBE system can automatically write an AML program to perform the task. While XPROBE is currently quite limited in the sorts of programs that it can write, it presents a very interesting alternative to the route taken in my research.

Another tool to aid in developing manipulator programs is off-line simulation ([Soroka 1980], EMULA [Meyer 1981]). Such a system allows the user to debug programs, at least roughly, without needing access to the actual manipulator which is often a scarce resource. The current level of simulation is still quite primitive, but is gradually increasing as factors such as sensing and dynamics begin to be included.

Programming Environments Work

When computers first came into use, time on them was a precious resource, and it was important to try to keep them busy all the time. On the other hand, the programmer's time was considered relatively inexpensive. This led to batch systems and off-line debugging (core dumps). Eventually the cost of computer time decreased, and the programmer's time became more important. This resulted in the use of timesharing systems, where programmers could interactively write and debug programs on-line. Currently computer cycles are cheap, and getting cheaper, while programming costs are climbing. A question now facing designers of software systems is how to best use the resources of the computer to aid the programmer in developing working programs. This section will describe several systems that have been developed to help the programmer.

The traditional tools used in developing programs have been text editors, compilers, linkers, loaders and debuggers. To get a working program the user was forced to run through an edit-compile-test cycle until the program was made to work. From the mid-seventies increasing attention has been focused on systems where these traditional tools are integrated into a single environment.

Lisp systems have a long history of providing a highly interactive programming environment [Sandewall 1978], a very successful example being Teitelman's Programmer's Assistant [Teitelman 1977]. This system makes extensive use of a bit map display screen and a pointing device (a mouse). A collection of display windows are used, one for each task, with the user being able to freely switch back and forth between them. The ability to suspend an operation, perform other operations, and then return without having destroyed the old context is quite helpful. Several special features of the system are the DWIM (for "Do What I Mean") automatic error correction facility, the ability to supply additional explanatory information after an error has occurred, and being able to point to any text on the screen and have the system treat it as input, i.e. as if it had just been typed in.

For more structured languages, such as Pascal or PL/I, a variety of systems have been developed. A key component of these systems is a special editor that has built-in knowledge of the programming language's syntax and semantics. The main idea is that by using one of these structure or syntax-directed editors, errors can be detected as the program is entered. There is no need to wait until an attempt is made to compile the program before identifying and correcting them. Since the editor understands the underlying structure of the program, editor commands can work directly on this structure. For example, when displaying the program the editor can show (i.e. prettyprint) this structure in varying levels of detail by replacing low-level portions with ellipsis marks. The statements elided can be automatically changed as the focus of the user shifts in the program [Mikelsons 1981], or this can be left for the user to do manually [Teitelbaum and Reps 1981]. One of the first structure-oriented editors for Pascal was MENTOR [Donzeau-Gouge 1975]. While most syntax-directed editors have been designed for a particular language, some are now being built to handle many different languages (BABEL [Horton 1981]).

Syntax-directed editors are template based, with different templates for each statement or expression in the language. Insertions to the program are made by invoking a routine to insert the appropriate template. In some systems the program is built as a parse tree with each statement or expression node entered with a separate command (IPE [Medina-Mora and Feiler 1981]), while in others special commands insert the statement templates, but expressions are entered as text (Cornell Program Synthesizer [Teitelbaum 1981]), and still others allow insertion of textual input for both statements and expressions, which is then immediately parsed and checked for syntactic correctness (COPE [Archer and Conway 1981], PDE1L [Mikelsons and Wegman 1980]).

Though syntax-directed editors have many advantages, particularly when used to aid in teaching programming, there are also a number of problems. For example, the prettyprinting method used is fixed, cramping the programmer's style. Also, since the program is required to be syntactically correct at all times, it can be difficult to make changes that would be simple with a standard text editor, e.g. transforming an IF statement into a WHILE loop.

The editor is only one part of the total programming environment. As the program develops the user will want to execute it, possibly while it is still in an incomplete state. Most programming environments have an interpreter for program testing, along with various debugging facilities (Cornell Program Synthesizer, COPE, PDE1L), though at least one such system is based on an incremental compiler (IPE). During execution, if a part of the program tree that has not been specified yet is reached, then execution will be suspended. The user can then use the editor to insert that section of the program. The editor will then either modify the internal parse tree used by the interpreter, or, for a compile-based system, recompile the modified section. Execution can then be resumed. Most of the various programming environments also allow the user to enter statements for immediate execution.

In addition to providing editing and debugging capabilities some systems also include facilities for both dynamic and static analysis of the program (LISPEDIT [Alberga et al. 1979]), or for aiding in program testing (PDE1L). Other systems have been designed to support the development of a program over its entire lifetime, from initial specifications (and their subsequent modification), to creation and editing of the program, through compilation, execution and debugging, on to system testing and evaluation, and finally to system maintenance (Programmer's Workbench [Ivie 1977], GANDALF [Habermann 1979], APSE [Buxton and Stenning 1980]).

Another, very ambitious direction is also being pursued whereby the computer would be a more active participant in the program development phase. An example of this approach is the Programmer's Apprentice [Rich and Shrobe 1978] where the user initially describes in high-level plans the task to be programmed. Then as the user instantiates these plans as actual code the system analyzes the code to see that it is consistent with the plans. If not, the system points out possible contradictions and omissions, and suggests how to correct them. While not automatic programming, this research is a step in that direction.

1.4 Brief Description of the AL Language

AL is an ALGOL-like language extended to handle the problems of manipulator control. The extensions include primitive data types to describe objects in a three-dimensional world, statements to specify the real-time motion of various devices, and the ability to execute statements in parallel. In this section a brief description of the AL language is provided. A very brief summary of the actual syntax is to be found in Appendix A. For a more complete treatment please refer to the "AL User's Manual" [Goldman and Mujtaba 1981].

Basic data types.   The basic data types in AL were chosen to facilitate working in the three dimensions of the real world. *Scalars* are floating point numbers; they correspond to *reals* in other programming languages. *Vectors* are a 3-tuple specifying (X, Y, Z) values, which represent either a translation or a location with respect to some coordinate system. *Rotations* are a 3 × 3 matrix representing either an orientation or a rotation about an axis. A *rotation*, or *rot*, is constructed from a vector, specifying the axis of rotation, and a scalar, giving the angle of rotation. *Frames* are used to represent local coordinate systems. They consist of a vector specifying the location of the origin, and a rotation specifying the orientation of the axes. *Transes* are used to transform frames and vectors from one coordinate system to another. Like frames they consist of a vector and a rotation. *Events* are used to coordinate processes run in parallel. *Arrays* are available for all of the above data types.

AL allows physical dimensions to be associated with variables. Some of the known dimensions include time, distance, angle, force, torque, velocity and angular velocity. New dimensions may be defined if desired. When parsing a program the system will check for consistent usage of dimensioned quantities in expressions and assignments.

Arithmetic operators.   Arithmetic operators exist to operate on these data types. Besides the familiar operations of addition, subtraction, multiplication, division, and exponentiation on reals, there are operators like vector dot and cross product, vector magnitude, composition of transformations, mapping from one coordinate system into another, plus a host of others. Basic boolean relational and logical operators are included, as are the normal trigonometric and scientific functions. There are also functions to build up *rotations, frames,* and *transes* from their component parts, as well as functions to extract those same component parts back again.

Basic control structures.   As mentioned above AL is an extension of ALGOL. As such it is block-structured; a program consists of a sequence of statements between a BEGIN-END pair. Variables must be declared before their use. AL has the traditional ALGOL control structures. These include:

```
IF <boolean condition> THEN <statement_ 1> ELSE <statement_ 2>
FOR <scalar variable> ← <exp> STEP <exp> UNTIL <exp> DO <statement>
WHILE <boolean condition> DO <statement>
DO <statement> UNTIL <boolean condition>
```

along with procedures, CASE statements and a statement to pause for a given time duration. Other familiar features include comments and macros.

Input/Output. AL has some input/output facilities. There is a PRINT statement, which knows about all the standard data types. The program can request input either of a scalar number or of a boolean value. It is also possible to have the program wait until the user enters a prompt character.

Parallel control. AL has the ability to execute several statements in "parallel." One way this is done is by putting them in a COBEGIN-COEND block. All statements in such a block are scheduled for simultaneous execution. The scheduling algorithm is to run the first statement until it blocks somehow (e.g. initiates a motion, pauses, etc.), then run the next. Synchronization between two processes is achieved with signal and wait primitives.

Another form of parallelism is possible with condition monitors. These consist of some condition, such as a boolean expression becoming true, a duration of time elapsing, or an event being signalled, and a statement to then execute. Condition monitors run at a higher priority than the main program and will interrupt it if the condition they are monitoring occurs.

Affixment. The spatial relationships between the various features of an object may be modelled by use of the AFFIX statement. AFFIX takes two frames and establishes a transformation between them. Whenever either of them is subsequently changed, the other will be updated to maintain the relationship that existed between them when they were affixed. Thus when an object is moved, all of its features will move with it. Variations of the affixment statement allow the value of the *trans* defining the relationship to be explicitly stated, or computed from the frames' current positions. The relationship can be broken by the UNFIX statement.

Motion control. There are, naturally, a variety of statements dealing with the control of external devices (e.g. manipulators). These statements can specify the device to be controlled, possibly along with a number of modifying clauses describing the desired motion. The MOVE statement is used to move an arm. Possible clauses include the destination location (this must be specified), any intermediate (VIA) points the motion should pass through, the speed with which the motion will take place, any forces to be applied, the stiffness characteristics of the arm, various conditions to monitor, and a host of others. The OPEN and CLOSE statements apply to hands and certain devices (e.g. a vise). Other devices (e.g. an electric socket driver) are controlled with the OPERATE statement. There is also a special CENTER statement for grasping objects which causes both the hand and arm to move together. The STOP statement allows a motion to be terminated before it has been completed.

Force control. During motions it is possible to specify the stiffness of the arm, and to both apply and sense forces. The STIFFNESS clause specifies the apparent stiffness of the object in the hand while following the specified trajectory. If the object encounters a constraining surface, then the contact force applied will depend on the stiffness coefficient along the direction of contact. A stiffness component of magnitude zero means that the arm will be compliant, i.e. move away from any external force in that direction. Also specified is the center of compliance about which the arm will comply.

In addition to stiffness control a force frame may be specified for a motion. The user may then apply a bias force or torque along any of the axes of this force frame. Also associated with the motion may be a condition monitor to sense forces and perform a given action if the magnitude of a force or torque crosses a specified threshold.

2

Problems of Manipulator Programming

This chapter examines some of the problems relating to manipulator programming. It first describes several of the difficulties that arise from including the physical world as a part of the programming environment and the consequent problems of programming in this environment. Then some specific issues relating to manipulator programming are discussed, such as object definition, motion control, use of force and compliance, error recovery, and parallelism. The chapter concludes by discussing the requirements for a successful manipulator programming environment in light of these problems.

2.1 The Effect of the Physical World

The physical environment for manipulator programming consists of one or more robot arms and various objects to be assembled along with possible jigs, fixtures, and parts feeders for them. There may also be other computer-controlled devices present, such as an electric socket driver or pneumatic vise.

When writing and debugging a manipulator program the user is attempting to effect deliberate changes in this physical world, which exists external to the computer. This creates a number of problems not found in more conventional computer programming. This section will examine some of the problems arising from this interaction.

Internal versus External Reality

An immediate consequence of dealing with objects external to the computer is that their state, which in this case primarily means position, must be modelled inside the computer. Moreover, this model must closely match that of the objects being modelled. Any discrepancies will result in activities such as the arm crashing into an object it thought was somewhere else, or the fingers attempting to grasp an object located just beyond their reach. While many other computer programs must also model the real world, errors in their models are not as immediately evident or embarrassing.

This correspondence between the internal model and external reality must be established for the program's initial state and must be maintained throughout its execution. When debugging the program, if the user wishes to restore the state to a prior condition to retry an operation, then not only must the internal computer model be reset, but also the physical objects in the robot's workspace must be repositioned. Likewise, if any of the objects are manually shifted, then the internal model had better be updated too. This is in contrast with more conventional programming where only the internal model, i.e. the program's variables, needs to be reset during debugging.

While the internal model is quite exact,[1] the correspondence of this model with the physical world is not as precise. A complication that arises is that there will be a certain degree of uncertainty in the internal model regarding the actual position of each object. For some objects, such as a fixture bolted to the workspace, this uncertainty will be extremely small, while for others it may be quite substantial. In dealing with those objects whose locations are not known exactly, it is essential to somehow refine the positional information. This can be done with sensing, e.g. vision or touch, or by making the manipulator compliant in an appropriate manner.

Besides the uncertainty inherent in each object's position, the manipulator itself is limited to a certain degree of accuracy. Very often steps in an assembly will require the manipulator to make motions requiring greater precision than it is capable of. A common example of this is inserting a pin in a hole where the clearance is an order of magnitude less than the positional accuracy of the arm. To further complicate matters, the manipulator's accuracy may vary over the workspace depending on its configuration.

Another, more positive aspect to working with real objects is that the user has immediate access to the current program state just by looking at where the objects and arms are. By watching the motion of the arms the flow of control in the program becomes obvious. Generally, any errors in the program will immediately manifest themselves to the user when that part of the program is reached. The user can then catch and repair them before proceeding with the remainder of the program.

Reversibility

In debugging a program, when a step is reached that does not work properly it is very useful to be able to back up and try it again, possibly after modifying the program. Backing up entails restoring the arm and objects being manipulated to the state they were in just prior to the failing step. In working with physical objects though, it is not always easy, or even possible, to undo an action. When a variable is internal to the computer the user can always modify its value using the appropriate debugging facilities, but some operations on physical objects are irreversible. Some examples are the operations of painting, riveting, drilling, or welding which cause a physical modification of the objects being manipulated.

To retry an operation, it may be necessary for the user to get a new copy of the object to replace the old modified one. Further it is likely that some of the operations just prior to the one being retried will also need to be repeated to establish the proper state required before the desired operation can be successfully retried.

There is another class of operations that are also difficult to reverse besides those causing physical modifications to the objects being manipulated. An example of this other type of operation is inserting a pin in a hole, which is fundamentally different from that of pulling the same pin out of the hole. The two operations involve similar force compliance strategies to avoid jamming the pin in the hole, but the manipulator will be compliant about different frames. Also, the insertion operation may involve finding the hole, which would not be a consideration when removing it. An even simpler example is the difference between just picking an object up off a surface and placing the same object down in contact with the surface. Picking up is a simple point to point motion, while placing down may need to make use of force sensing to determine when contact has been made.

Context Sensitivity

A standard approach to writing a large computer program is to develop small pieces of it individually and then to put them together into larger chunks, eventually resulting in a completed program, i.e. bottom up programming. For this method to work it is essential that the small pieces of code be relatively insensitive to the code that precedes them and that there are no hidden assumptions concerning the context within which the code occurs. For manipulator programming this is often not the case; code which worked reliably when tested in isolation frequently fails when placed in the context of the larger program.

There are two general classes of assumptions that become embedded in the user's code: those that arise due to changes in manipulator geometry as it is moved from location to location, and those that crop up when the rate at which an operation is performed is changed. These will be further discussed below.

Location dependencies. Manipulator code is highly sensitive to initial conditions, especially the initial arm position. For trajectories based on splining, the starting position will influence the trajectory that will be used for the motion. The initial arm position may also influence the velocity with which the arm will be moving during some critical part of the motion. While these effects can be dealt with by using more complicated motion statements, the problem may not arise until after the initial code has been debugged in isolation and is joined with the code preceding it.

Code written to perform an operation at one location is likely to need to be tuned to make it work at a different location. Changes in location will result in changes in the manipulator's geometry. Moving the manipulator to the new location at best results in only changing the manipulator's accuracy, inertial characteristics, sensitivity and delicacy. At worst it may change the arm's configuration, e.g. from left shouldered to right, or flip a wrist. Moreover, this change in configuration may occur during what had previously been a simple motion.

If trajectories are computed in joint space,[2] then even very similar small motions may be subtly different. For example, sliding along a surface at one location may result in a trajectory that curves into the surface, exerting extra pressure on it, while motion at another nearby location may curve away from the surface, reducing the pressure and possibly losing contact with it. Specifying that the manipulator apply a bias force perpendicular to the surface can be used to solve this particular example, but such a surface will not always be present. The ability to make straight line motions in Cartesian space would, of course, cause this problem to disappear, but would introduce other problems such as ragged motions near singularities of the manipulator.

The manipulator's geometry also affects the delicacy of forces that may be applied with it. At one location the primary joint chosen to exert a given force may be very close to the hand, while for another position the appropriate joint may be very far from the hand, resulting in a longer, more massive lever arm which will be less accurate at controlling forces [Salisbury and Craig 1981].

Speed dependencies. When testing a motion for the first time it is often wise to have the manipulator move slowly. This allows the user a chance to interrupt the motion if it appears to be about to cause a collision. It also allows the user to closely inspect the motion. After the motion has undergone some initial debugging at a slower speed it is then desirable to speed things up. In doing so many aspects of the motion will change.

Increasing the speed may introduce a different trajectory if a splining method is used. The main problem here is that overshooting will be more likely. The resulting trajectory will also be more apt to wander further away from the straight lines connecting the end and intermediate points of the motion. This may or may not cause complications.

More likely to be a problem is that different forces will occur whenever the arm is in contact with anything. Moreover, due to the increased speed, these forces will be greater and tend to build up more quickly. If the forces are too large, damage may be done to either the arm, the object it is holding, or whatever is bumped into. Also, any object held in the hand is liable to be shifted, making its position uncertain thereafter.

With higher force levels that rapidly build up, the force compliance system may be called on to respond faster than it is able to. As a result, operations which had succeeded at a slower speed may no longer work. For example, a previously successful insertion operation may now result in jamming.

How these changes in force might affect an assembly operation can be seen by considering a motion used in trying to locate a hole. The arm is holding a pin-like object and sliding it along a surface. When the pin passes over the hole it will drop into it slightly, and an increased force along the direction of motion will occur when the pin hits the far edge of the hole. When this extra force is sensed the arm is halted, while the pin is still in the hole.

If this operation is sped up, then a number of changes will occur. First, the sliding motion will not be as smooth, which will increase the noise level of the signal from the force sensors, causing the threshold for sensing contact to be increased. Next, the pin will not have time to drop as far into the hole, resulting in it making less contact with the far edge, which means less contact force to be sensed. However, the increased velocity with which contact will be made will also tend to increase this force. Whether this will compensate for the decrease due to less of the pin making contact is unclear. Finally, assuming that the contact force is above the noise level, the increased speed of the motion gives the servo less time to react and stop the arm before the pin is pulled past the hole.

Other Points

Many of the above problems are due to the current performance limitations of manipulator servo control. Much current active research is aimed at increasing the abilities of servo control systems and adding new capabilities to them. However, there always will be upper limits on manipulator performance, and programming tasks which will need abilities in excess of those limits.

Another effect of the above mentioned context sensitivity is that libraries and generalized procedures are very difficult. It is essential to insulate the code from the various initial conditions that will no doubt be encountered. Besides the effect of position and speed dependencies other problems can arise. For example, changing the size of the objects will have an uncertain, but definite effect; any scaling will undoubtedly result in different forces being encountered and will require different stiffness values to be set.

2.2 Specific Manipulator Programming Issues

The previous section discussed some of the general types of problems that arise from dealing with the physical world. This section will focus in on some of the more specific problems that must be faced in writing and debugging manipulator programs. Particular attention will be paid to how these problems manifest themselves in AL programs. Related discussions can be found in [Finkel 1976] and [Taylor 1976].

Defining Objects

One of the first problems that must be dealt with in performing an assembly is to model the relevant features of the objects being assembled and to enter this information into the manipulator program. For each object two pieces of information are usually necessary. First, the initial location of the object must somehow be specified. Second, the spatial relationship between any features of the object must be defined.

Specifying the location of an object entails giving both its position (a vector) and its orientation (a rotation) with respect to some previously defined coordinate system. These two components may be either constants or expressions based on other variables. They may be exactly known or they may need to be determined by some form of sensing, e.g. touch or vision.

While the object itself has a three-dimensional shape and a volume, the object's location is just an oriented point in space. This point is used to define the origin of a coordinate system for the object. Other features of the object that play a part in the assembly can then be described with respect to this coordinate system. When the object is moved in space these features will need to move with it. Examples of common features of typical objects include: a grasping point for gripping the object with the fingers of a manipulator, a point on a surface of the object used to mate against another surface, and screw holes.

For AL programs this information takes the form of a series of declaration, assignment and affixment statements. The declaration statements are used to associate a variable with each object. The assignment statements are used to assign a frame constant holding the object's initial position to this variable. The affixment statements are used to define the relative positions of the object's features to each other.[3] For typical AL programs these initialization statements make up 20–40 percent of the program [Grossman and Taylor 1975].

Somehow the user must acquire the necessary information to model the objects and incorporate it into the appropriate declaration, assignment and affixment statements. There are several different ways in which this might be done. Ideally all of the objects would already have been modelled by some computer aided design (CAD) system and a special program would convert the model into the relevant AL statements either automatically or based on interactive commands from the user. Unfortunately such a program to make use of existing models has yet to be written.

Also, even if such a program did exist, the objects being manipulated may not have been modelled in a CAD system. The same applies to any fixtures involved and to the location of objects and fixtures in the manipulator's workspace. In the case where the model does not exist, or is incomplete, entering all of the information necessary to build up a complete volumetric model for the purpose of then extracting a few positional values would seem to be a case of overkill. Eventually, of course, vision systems will be capable of building up the necessary models from several views of the objects and the workspace [Nevatia and Binford 1973].

Another approach at the opposite extreme is for the user to manually measure the objects with a ruler and protractor, and then use a text editor to enter the needed statements. While this method will work, it can be very tedious and error prone.

In particular, determining orientations is quite difficult for all but the simplest cases.

A third way is to use the manipulator itself as a measuring tool to determine the positions of the objects and of their features. As the information for each object is obtained it can then be put into AL statements, either directly by the program being used to move the manipulator, manually by the user, or some combination of the two. At Stanford a system employing this method, called POINTY [Goldman and Mujtaba 1981], has been used to successfully speed up the object definition step.

If the manipulator is used for measurement, it is important that it be easy for the user to move it about. For small arms it may be safe for the user to actually grab the arm and physically move it to the desired location. The arm may either be actively servoed to be compliant while the user moves it, or it may be limp, i.e. with its brakes released. For the user to come in physical contact with larger manipulators may be dangerous though. Another convenient method to manually position a manipulator is to use a joystick or teach box.[4] While sometimes slower than manually wrestling the arm into place, a joystick or teach box offers greater control over the motion, possibly restricting it to a single axis or joint. Even greater control is offered by the symbolic instructions in the manipulator programming language, though entering them may be more time consuming.

The above discussion has been concerned with creating a new model for the initial situation. It is also essential to be able to define new objects and modify old ones during program debugging. Any errors which had been made when creating the model will need to be corrected. Also, if any changes had been made to the objects or their fixtures, this must be incorporated into the model. The user may need to introduce auxiliary locations both for aspects of the model which had been overlooked when the model was first created and for temporary use during debugging.

Modification of an existing model is also necessary when changing an old, already debugged program so it will work for either a differently configured workspace, i.e. the objects and fixtures have been shifted about, or for slightly different objects.

Gross versus Fine Motions

Manipulator motions can be divided into two broad classes. Gross motions are those which move the manipulator over a large distance, usually fairly quickly. They are in contrast with fine motions where a great deal of attention is spent in moving the manipulator a small distance. Gross motions are used to move about the workspace, while fine motions are used for operations such as parts mating. Often a motion statement in a program will combine an initial gross motion with a final fine motion, or vice versa.

In general, gross motions present few problems for the manipulator programmer. Current manipulator systems are sufficiently advanced that when commanded to go from one point to another, they will. The programmer needs to consider two potential problem areas though.

First, collision avoidance is the user's responsibility. The manipulator system has no knowledge of the volume objects occupy and is as likely to attempt to move through an object or fixture as to go around it. Detecting potential collisions is relatively straightforward, though it sometimes requires quick reflexes on the user's part. Adding intermediate points to the motion specification to avoid the collisions is also easy, though if it is desired that the motion takes the minimal time, then their placement can be nontrivial.

A second related problem is that the manipulator may need to change its configuration[5] during a large motion. If the destination of the motion cannot be reached in the manipulator's starting configuration it may be necessary to switch to another one. When the manipulator flips its wrist, changes elbow orientation, or switches from right shouldered to left, it will sweep out a path quite different from that of the line between its starting and destination locations. This motion is almost always a surprise to the programmer and is often apt to cause a collision. There is no clear cut solution to this problem except to add statements to the program to explicitly change the arm configuration, and to do so in a safe location where no collisions will occur. If the new configuration can also reach the starting point of the motion, then it may be better to change the configuration one or several motions earlier. For example, if the arm were moving a liquid in a glass, then flipping the wrist would likely result in the liquid spilling out. Instead it would be necessary to change configurations before picking the glass up. Sometimes this problem can be avoided by changing the orientation of the destination position so that the initial configuration can be used to reach it. This is often possible when the object being moved has an axis of symmetry about which the orientation is irrelevant. For example consider a screw or bolt, or the glass mentioned above.

Changes in configuration can also occur during fine motions, but this is much less likely since the manipulator is moving in a small volume. If the position is close to a joint limit though, then a configuration change may result. The solution here is to either relocate the working volume somewhere where the arm has a greater range of movement, or to change configurations earlier. Often changing the way that the manipulator is grasping the object will solve the problem.

A major use of fine motions is in parts mating. To put two objects together requires the manipulator to correctly position the object it is holding with respect to the other object. This is more than just a point to point motion, however. The path that the manipulator takes often needs to avoid premature contact between the objects, that is the non-mating surfaces of the objects must not bump into each other. Consequently the final part of the motion is usually along a normal to the surfaces being mated.

The first step involved in programming a parts-mating operation is to define the necessary final and intermediate points. The final point can be computed from the models of the two objects, though it is often easier to manually shift the manipulator holding the object to the correct position and record its location.[6] Likewise, values for intermediate points can be assigned, either when the motion statement is first written or, more likely, after an unwanted collision has occurred in testing the motion.

In addition to the attention focused on the path the object is moved along, parts mating also relies heavily on force sensing and compliance. Due to uncertainty concerning the objects' locations, force sensing is often required to detect when contact between the objects occurs. Some form of active compliance is needed for operations such as inserting a pin or bolt in a hole where tolerances are apt to be smaller than the manipulator's absolute accuracy or where the various uncertainties, such as the position of the hole and the location of the pin in the hand, are too great. Force sensing and compliance will be discussed in the next section.

A single parts-mating operation may require several motion statements, making up an assembly strategy. For example, inserting a pin in a hole might first involve finding the surface surrounding the hole, and then sliding across the surface to locate the hole. Next, the orientation of the pin might be shifted from one suited for finding the hole, to one parallel to the axis of the hole. Finally, a compliant motion to insert the pin in the hole would complete the operation. Taylor provides an extensive discussion of the pin-in-hole operation [Taylor 1976].

To program a successful parts-mating operation, then, requires both specifying the proper trajectory and setting the correct thresholds and levels for force sensing and compliance. This is currently very difficult to do without actually trying out the motion with the manipulator and debugging/tuning the various parameters. In fact, most of the time taken to write a manipulator program is spent in dealing with fine motions.

Force and Compliance

Many assembly operations require some form of force sensing or active force control. As has been mentioned this is due to the uncertainty inherent in working with objects in the real world combined with the limitations on the accuracy of the manipulator. Being able to sense and apply forces greatly extends the class of operations that the manipulator is capable of performing successfully.

The simplest example of force sensing is detecting when the manipulator, or an object being held by it, comes in contact with a surface. Conversely it is possible to detect contact being lost when the force vanishes. Contact can be maintained when moving along a surface by exerting a bias force along a vector normal to the surface.

When doing an insertion it is important to be able to alter the manipulator's stiffness so that it is compliant in the plane perpendicular to the hole, but stiff along the axis of the hole. Controlling the stiffness is also needed when sliding along a surface or edge. In both cases it is useful to be able to vary the location of the frame which the manipulator is compliant about. The former should be compliant about the tip of the object being inserted, while the latter should be compliant about a point on the sliding object where it is in contact with the stationary surface.

Another example of force sensing is weighing an object that has been picked up by the manipulator. This may be done when the manipulator is stationary or while it is in motion, though this can be difficult if the object is being accelerated.

A number of problems arise when programming motions that involve force. The first of these is that there is no easy relation between vague terms like *gently, lightly,* and *heavily* and the strict numeric values used by the manipulator programming language. For detecting contact the programmer wishes to say something like "stop when contact is made," but the language requires a force threshold value that will stop the motion when exceeded. Merely choosing a small number for this threshold will not always work since the threshold must be greater than any possible noise values generated during the motion. The range of the noise will depend on the manipulator's configuration, the load being moved, and the accelerations applied during the motion.

The forces generated during an operation like contact depend on the load being carried by the manipulator and on the manipulator's velocity at contact. When sliding one object alongside another, the force will be affected by the texture of the opposing surfaces, the downwards pressure applied, and the velocity of the motion.

Getting the desired motion requires proper values for force thresholds, manipulator stiffness, compliant frame location, and manipulator velocity to be chosen. This involves making an educated guess for the initial values, then trying out the motion and subsequently tuning the various parameters. This brings out another major problem in that the forces which occur during a motion are invisible to the programmer; at best they can be observed indirectly if the manipulator lurches around or slams into something.

If the programmer is to be able to intelligently modify the various force parameters, then it is essential that the forces arising during the motion be made visible somehow: some sort of graphics display is called for. The user will need to compare both different force components in the same motion and also the same force components as a motion is repeated. At the end of the next chapter several examples involving force will be given showing such a force-graphics capability in use.

Many of the above problems stem from the fact that current manipulators are still very crude when it comes to working with force. Almost always the programmer is forced to work at the limits of the manipulator's sensitivity and delicacy. This problem will persist until force capabilities have improved by several orders of magnitude, and even then it will not go away entirely—there will always be tasks with performance requirements that exceed available capabilities.

Another important use of graphic force feedback is by the implementers and maintainers of a manipulator programming system. In working with the force control section of the arm servo, when either adding a new feature or tracking down a suspected bug, it is essential for the manipulator systems programmer to have a way of meaningfully inspecting both the desired[7] and actual performance of the manipulator. This allows the control method underlying the force servoing to be confirmed and is the only way the servo can be tuned for best operation of the actual manipulator. Being able to view the force data graphically is a straightforward way of determining that the force system indeed works as it is supposed to.

Graphic feedback of other motion parameters not related to force, such as the difference between the planned and actual trajectory, is also a great aid for tuning and debugging other aspects of the arm servo by the manipulator systems programmer. It is sometimes possible to check the gross behavior of the arm servo by watching the motion of the manipulator; for example, feedback on Cartesian straight line motion can be gathered by observing the manipulator skim along a flat surface. More dynamic aspects of the motion tend to be harder to observe. If the manipulator's actual motion were consistently lagging behind the arm servo's desired path, possibly due to an incorrect model of the arm in the servo or to a problem in the hardware, it would be very difficult to identify the problem, or even notice that it was a problem, without being able to examine data collected during the motion. A special diagnostic program (called DIAGY) has been used at Stanford for just this purpose. It has been used to both tune and debug the arm servo, and also to diagnose bugs in the hardware when the arm starts to act flaky.

Parallelism

Parallelism arises quite naturally in manipulator programming. During an assembly the user is apt to make use of several manipulators, their associated hands, and various auxiliary devices or tools. At occasional times in the course of the assembly it will likely be desired to have operations involving these devices overlap. There are several ways this concurrency will occur. Some of these operations will be totally independent—that is, asynchronous, joined only at their start and conclusion. A simple example of this is driving in a screw by operating an electric screw driver while the arm is pressing down. A large number will be loosely coupled— that is, basically asynchronous, but needing to coordinate activities at certain points. An example is passing an object from one manipulator to another. In AL this coordination is done through the use of semaphore primitives which signal and wait for special event variables. Finally, some will be tightly coupled, such as two arms cooperatively carrying one object.

Another use of parallelism is to monitor for a condition becoming true as the program is being executed. At some point in the program this condition monitor is enabled, and it will run in parallel with the normal execution, waiting for the desired condition to occur. Associated with the monitor is code which will be executed if the condition becomes true. When a later point in the program is reached, checking will be disabled and the condition monitor deactivated. The scope of the condition monitor may be a single statement, for example checking for a force to indicate contact during a motion, or a larger section of the program.

The use of the above mentioned parallelism can create several different types of problems for the user. The most common of these arises when avoiding collisions between the various active manipulators. The user can generally foresee potential collisions between one manipulator and the stationary objects in the workspace, but this becomes much more difficult when several arms are swinging back and forth through the same portion of the workspace. To avoid the manipulators crashing into each other, the appropriate processes need to be coupled such that only one of them is using the common region of the workspace at any given time. This is an example of the more general resource-sharing problem, where the resource in this case is empty space. Other resource-sharing may occur when two processes both make use of the same manipulator or device.

Once the problem is recognized, which is usually not until after the program has been executed at least once, a solution can be achieved by inserting SIGNAL and WAIT statements into the appropriate points in the interfering processes to provide an interlock. Of course this can then introduce other problems, such as deadlocking, where each process is waiting for the other.

Since some assembly operations may take a variable amount of time, race conditions may arise. For example, during the debugging phase one process may always finish before another, while during actual program execution this order may be reversed. This could result in a collision if the first process depended on finishing first to give it time to move the manipulator it is controlling out of the way of the one controlled by the second process. Such race conditions may not show up until after a program has undergone extensive testing.

For loosely coupled processes an interlock is also required to synchronize the associated processes at certain points. Again the user must first identify the points in the processes where synchronization is needed, and then insert the appropriate SIGNAL and WAIT statements.

The average AL user to date has had little prior experience in coping with parallel processes and consequently has difficulty putting in appropriate SIGNAL and WAIT statements. Usually this difficulty takes the form of using too many of them (but still occasionally missing the crucial point), and in introducing deadlock by interchanging the order of the SIGNAL and WAIT statements in a process—that is, waiting for another process to complete some action before having signalled that same process that it is safe to proceed. It is important for the manipulator programming environment to offer some form of assistance to help users deal with parallelism. At the least such a system should make it easy to recover from a deadlock and to determine why the deadlock occurred.

Another difficulty arises once the appropriate SIGNAL and WAIT statements have been added to the program. In addition to running the program as a whole, the user is likely to wish to run a single process by itself in order to debug it. This presents a problem since the process will halt whenever it encounters a WAIT statement, but the process which would have signalled the appropriate event to cause it to continue will not be running. The user will need some way of getting around this difficulty either by manually signalling the event or ignoring the WAIT statement.

Error Recovery

A direct consequence of working with the physical world is that objects may not be exactly where they should be and hence motions that deal with them may fail. Part of manipulator programming involves attempting to take this into account and making assembly operations as robust as possible. Even so, errors are likely, and another aspect of manipulator programming must be to recover from these errors.

Almost any motion statement in the user's program can fail, sometimes for a variety of reasons. Some of the more common manipulator errors are: objects shifting or dropping out of the hand, an object missing from where it should be, jamming during an insertion, not being able to locate a hole, etc.

The first problem that arises for error recovery is identifying that an error has indeed occurred. This will likely be very evident to the programmer, who *knows* what should be happening and can *see* the assembly. The manipulator system, however, has no such knowledge and usually no visual facilities. For it to detect the error the program must contain some type of explicit test. This test might involve checking the manipulator's position to see that it lies in the proper range; for example, when doing an insertion, no change in position might indicate jamming, while too much change might indicate that the hole was missed entirely or that the object being inserted has slipped out of the hand. Other checks might involve force, such as weighing the load being carried to check that the object is still there and has not been dropped, or checking that a contact force remains relatively constant during a motion. If the manipulator system has some type of visual capabilities then it might take a picture and check for the presence or absence of an object, and, if the object is present, determine its location.

Since every motion statement in the program may potentially fail, these explicit checks can be quite cumbersome and take up more space than the rest of the program. Rather than attempt to deal with all possible errors, which would be a herculean task, as the program is being written and tested out, those statements which are observed to fail can be singled out and explicit error checking added to them.

Once an error has been detected, an attempt can be made to recover from it. This can be done totally by the manipulator under program control, or may involve manual intervention by the user, or some combination of the two. In any event, the recovery attempt may in turn result in new errors. It is easy to see how code to recover from errors can become the major part of the manipulator program.

In addition to the problem of detecting and recovering from errors in a working manipulator program, there is also the problem of coping with errors during the debugging process as the program is being written. When an error occurs during debugging the programmer may wish either to retry the failing operation or just to continue with the next statement in the program. To retry an operation it is necessary to back the program up so that the state of the world is restored to what it was before the motion that failed. Before continuing execution it will likely be necessary to fix whatever had failed. In both cases this will involve moving the manipulator to a new position and repositioning the various objects involved in the assembly. While some of this will be done manually by the user, it will also be desirable to be able to use the manipulator for other parts. As noted at the beginning of this chapter, when any object is repositioned the internal model will also need to be updated.

The use of parallelism in manipulator programs can further complicate recovery from errors. When several processes are running concurrently and one causes an error to occur, it may or may not affect the other processes. In many cases the programmer will wish to back up the offending process, while allowing the others to continue. Other times it will be necessary to reset several or all of the running processes.

2.3   Requirements of a Manipulator Programming Environment

One of the major facts that should be apparent from the preceding discussion is that manipulator programming is a highly interactive task. To debug the program, the user will need to be able to try out parts of it, make changes to them, and then try them out again. Any system for manipulator program development will need to provide support for the user in this and the other activities mentioned in the previous sections. This section will attempt to sketch out the requirements for a successful manipulator programming environment in the light of these and other problems.

How Manipulator Programs Are Written

When writing an AL manipulator program, people at Stanford have tended to follow a characteristic pattern. Before starting to write their program they have a fairly good idea of the steps that will be required for the particular assembly being performed and the order in which those steps should be executed. This description of the assembly is at the task level, and it is usually expressed as how the programmer would go about performing the assembly using human arms, rather than computer-controlled robot arms. If fixtures or jigs are to be used, they have already been designed and built. The user usually, though not always, has a rough idea of how the workspace will be organized, but this is just a sketch, not an exact positioning of the various objects, their fixtures, and where each assembly operation will take place. Sometimes a geometric model of the various objects and fixtures has been obtained from measurements or written specifications.

The first on-line step in developing the program is to build up the information needed for the internal model. Using the manipulator as a measuring tool and a special program, called POINTY, the user proceeds to define the features of the various objects and fixtures, resulting in a series of affixment statements at the start of the developing AL program. At this time the actual locations of the objects in the workspace are determined by the user, and this information is placed in assignment statements.

Next, the user will start programming the individual steps which make up the assembly. These will be dealt with separately, the user refining the initial attempt at programming the manipulator to do each step until a successful sequence of statements is achieved. This in turn may be further improved to make the operation sufficiently robust.

To achieve a working piece of code for a given step, the user will normally start out with a sequence of absolute motion statements, which, when tried, will almost work, but will have some definite bugs. Modifying the fine motion sections by defining and adding new intermediate points is the usual first step taken to correct matters. The purpose of these intermediate points is mainly to eliminate unwanted collisions, and to specify the direction that the manipulator is moving at a given point in the motion. If this is not sufficient then various motion clauses to sense or apply forces will next be added. The parameters of these force clauses will then need to be tuned. More experienced users may include force clauses right from the start.

Once several steps have been successfully programmed they can be put together and any interference between them eliminated. Possible interference can usually be dealt with by minor modifications of the existing motion statements, or by adding additional motion statements between the steps. Occasionally more major alterations are required, for example, if the manipulator's configuration needs to be changed.

After the tasks for each manipulator have been written and debugged separately, the programmer may then combine them to run concurrently. This involves adding statements to coordinate the parallel operations. This coordination is needed both where the user deliberately desires the arms to cooperate and wherever they have conflicting needs, for example, where they might collide. Debugging any problems introduced by the parallelism can be very tedious. To retry an operation may involve backing up and restoring the state for several processes. Also, the amount of code involved can be quite large, which complicates the checking needed for detecting any possible interference between the various parallel processes. The code may need to be run for some time before the interference becomes apparent.

In summary, programs are developed in a basically bottom up manner: first, a model of the objects in the workspace is built up, then each of the individual assembly operations is programmed using fine motions, which are then combined in larger and larger sections, and, finally, these sections may be made to run concurrently. Most of the time spent in writing and debugging a manipulator program takes place in defining the required locations and in the debugging of the manipulator motions for the individual assembly steps.

Requirements in Common with Conventional Programming

As the manipulator program is being developed, the debugging process involved requires the same sorts of tools as are used for debugging conventional computer programs. A flexible editing facility is needed to allow the user to make additions and modifications to the developing program. Various debugging facilities are needed to control program execution and to allow the user to examine and modify the current state.

The editor must support the user during writing and debugging the manipulator program. One form for this support is allowing the user to easily modify an existing statement. This is a very common activity when tuning the parameters for a motion. To minimize typing mistakes, the amount of retyping should be kept to a minimum, and the user should immediately see the effect of the changes on the program. It should also be easy to insert and delete motion clauses or statements. Ideally, some form of display editor will be used, providing the user a window into the program.

When modifying the program it would be quite helpful for the editor to check that the changes do not violate the syntax of the manipulator language. If they do, then the user should be informed of the syntactic errors and allowed to correct them. When a change is made in the program, the editor needs to either automatically recompile it or, if an interpreter is used, translate it into the appropriate internal representation. If a compile-based system is used it must be possible to recompile and reload sections of the program without disturbing the dynamic information associated with the current execution state. The editor must be an integral part of the execution and debugging environment.

The debugging facilities should include the ability to set and clear breakpoints in the program. During program execution if a breakpoint is encountered then execution will be suspended and control passed to the user through the debugger. It must also be possible to subsequently proceed with the program's execution. Some form of single stepping capability is also very useful. When the program is temporarily suspended it is important that the user can determine where the break occurred, and how control had reached that point. This tracing information should also describe the status of all the processes which are currently active.

It is also necessary to be able to change the order of program execution, for example, going back and re-executing several statements which had just failed and then been subsequently modified. The ability to immediately execute statements entered directly by the user, and not part of the program, is also extremely desirable.

The user must be able to examine the current values of the various variables and be able to modify these values. It is also useful to be able to evaluate algebraic expressions involving the program and system variables and to be able to use such expressions when assigning a new value to a variable.

As mentioned above, it is vital that the user be able to modify the currently running program with the editor without affecting the runtime environment. The debugger, editor, and runtime system should form a single programming environment.

A Proposed Manipulator Environment

By putting all of the above requirements together, a picture begins to emerge of what a manipulator programming environment should look like. The user should be able to enter single statements for immediate execution, or use an editor to create a manipulator program for future execution. Programs can be debugged and modified on-line. Special debugging features should exist such as breakpoints, and single-stepping, altering control flow, displaying gathered force data, examining and changing variables, etc. The debugging facilities should also be able to cope with parallel processes and help the user deal with this concurrency.

Another design goal is for the resulting system to be portable so it can be exported to other robotics projects. Also making the system capable of being distributed over several computers is desirable. At Stanford, future systems will use several processors: one for the interpreter and one for manipulator servo control. Eventually each manipulator will have one or more processors dedicated to controlling it.

A system satisfying the above requirements, allowing manipulator programs to be written, modified, debugged, and run in a single environment, would provide an efficient man-machine interface between the programmer and the manipulators. Such an interactive system is described in the next chapter.

3

The AL System

This chapter describes the interactive AL manipulator programming environment from the user's viewpoint and attempts to show how it facilitates the creation, debugging and running of manipulator programs. It describes the interpreter, the syntax-directed editor, the debugging facilities, and the force graphics subsystem. Examples are given showing how the system works in actual operation.

3.1 Overview

The initial implementation of AL consisted of a compiler and a separate runtime interpreter. These ran on different machines: the compiler on SAIL's DEC KL10, and the runtime system on a PDP-11/45. To create a working AL program the user first entered the text of the program using the standard system editor (E [Samuel 1980]). This was then compiled, possibly several times, until all syntactic errors had been eliminated. The resulting object code was then down-loaded onto the runtime machine. It was then tested and any bugs present in the program were hopefully identified. This edit-compile-debug loop would then be repeated until the program did what the user wanted it to.

To speed up this process a program called POINTY was developed. POINTY offered the user a limited interactive capability that greatly facilitated program development. It was initially designed to assist the users by letting them use the manipulator itself in building up the spatial relations—that is, the relative locations and their attachments—of the objects and fixtures used in an assembly. The resulting definitions could be saved in a file and later edited into an AL program. Over the years POINTY evolved to look more and more like an interpreter for AL. This allowed statements to be tried out on-line, again helping to minimize the time needed for program development. However, the POINTY system suffered from a number of problems. The most notable of these was that POINTY did not provide any editing facilities to enable the user to interactively modify the AL program being developed. Also, since POINTY ran on the DEC KL10 and communicated with the AL runtime system on the PDP-11/45 there was a problem with the low bandwidth between the two machines.

Another part of the old AL system was a special subsystem developed to provide the ability to graphically display force information gathered during the course of a motion. This module, called GAL, ran on the DEC KL 10 and communicated with the runtime system on the PDP-11/45. After a motion had occurred, GAL would read in the gathered force data and, using SAIL's graphics capabilities, allow the user to display it in a number of different ways. By providing feedback to the user concerning the forces occurring during the motion, the debugging of more complicated motions and force strategies was facilitated.

After working with AL, POINTY, and GAL it became obvious that the next step was to develop an interactive AL system running on a single machine that would allow users to edit, run, and debug their programs in a single environment. Furthermore this system should be written to be as portable as possible.

This next AL system is the subject of the rest of this book. It consists of an interpreter, a structure display editor, debugging facilities, and an arm servo module. The user interacts with the AL system primarily through the editor. Besides being used to enter and modify the user's AL program, the editor is also used to invoke the interpreter and debugging facilities. The interpreter communicates with the arm servo module to control the manipulators and other devices.

3.2   Editor

The editor is the main interface between the user and the AL system. The user's AL program is entered and modified by the editor. It is also through the editor that the user talks to the debugger and then to the interpreter. The editor used in the AL system is a structure display editor. "Structure" means that it has built-in knowledge about the syntax of the AL language. It also means that the user's program is always guaranteed to be syntactically correct, though possibly incomplete. Being a display editor it uses the entire screen for editing. The editor is strongly influenced by the E display editor used on SAIL. Also associated with the editor is a line editor similar to the one used on SAIL. The editor is designed to be run on a standard CRT terminal with fairly minimal display features.

This section discusses the editor from the user's viewpoint. The available editor commands are described and several examples using the editor to create and modify a sample AL program are shown. The next chapter will cover the editor's internal details, along with how the various operations are performed.

The editor divides the screen into two parts: a window into the current program, and below it a smaller region which echoes user commands. Any type-out from the user's program also appears in this echo window. The size of the echo window can be varied by the user. Surrounding the window into the program are a header and trailer line giving information about the program's size and location of the current window in the program. For example, while editing a small program the display screen might look like:

```
***** Line    1 *********************
BEGIN
SCALAR i, j;
j := 0;
PRINT("Starting - ");
FOR i := 1 STEP 1 UNTIL 5 DO
    BEGIN
    j := j + i;
    PRINT(i);
    END;
PRINT(" = ",j);
> END
***** Cursor at Line   11 of   11 *****
OK ↑S OK
run
Starting - 1 2 3 4 5 =   15
ALL DONE   OK
```

In the above example the user had typed the commands: ↑S and run. Everything else was a system response. When displaying the program, the editor prettyprints it automatically.

Editor Commands

Editor commands come in two flavors: commonly used commands involving a single keystroke and less frequently used ones requiring an entire word to be typed (extended commands). When entering extended commands the user is talking to a line editor which allows flexibility in correcting any typographical errors. The line editor is described in the next subsection. The single-keystroke commands are either control characters (e.g. ↑B, ↑I, etc.) or otherwise special characters (e.g. ⟨space⟩, ⟨cr⟩, ⟨tab⟩, "<", etc.). Many single keystroke editor commands can take a numeric argument. This value is given by typing a ↑\ followed by the number. For example,↑\ 23↑L would move the cursor to line 23.

When the editor is first started it contains a "null" program consisting of a single BEGIN-END block. The user can either enter the program using the commands given below, or request the system to read in a previously prepared AL program from a file. To read in a program one uses the extended command GET followed by the name of the file. For example to read in the file FOO.AL, one would type "GET FOO.AL". The system would then read and parse the contents of the file, printing out any syntactic errors encountered in the echo window. Included in the editor is a prettyprinter which formats the program for proper display. While reading in a program the echo window size is automatically extended to a maximal size so any error messages won't immediately disappear. After the program has been read in, the echo window reverts to its previous size. The echo window size can be manually adjusted with the extended command SET BOTSIZE ⟨number⟩.

At the end of a session, or any other time, the user can write out the program, as it currently exists, to a specified file with the SAVE command followed by the file name, e.g. "SAVE demo1.al". Note: this only saves the text of the program; the current value of various variables and any affixments are not saved. When totally done, the system is exited with ↑E.

There are a number of commands to shift the window into the program. To move down one screenful use ↑W. ↑U moves up one screenful. To roll the screen up or down by 4 lines one uses ↑B and ↑T. To move the cursor line to the top of the screen one uses ↑P. ↑\-↑P moves the cursor to the bottom of the screen. If the screen is ever garbaged for some reason, ↑V will redraw it and the current echo window.

To move the cursor down or up one line one uses ⟨cr⟩ and ⟨bs⟩. ">" and "<" move it down or up by 4 lines. The cursor can be positioned at a given line by ↑\<number>↑L. If no argument is given, i.e. ↑L, then the cursor is moved to the first line of the program. When the cursor is moved by more than 4 lines the editor "remembers" the old position and one can move back to this old line with ↑O.

In addition to moving the cursor by lines, the editor knows how to move by AL statements. ↑S will move the cursor down to the start of the next statement, descending into block structure if possible. That is, if the cursor were pointing at a FOR statement then ↑S would reposition it at the body of the FOR statement. Similarly if it were pointing at a BEGIN statement ↑S would move the cursor to the first statement in the block. This differs from ↑N which also moves down one statement, but stays at the current lexical level. So if the cursor was again pointing at a FOR statement, then ↑N would move it to the next statement following it, not at the body of the FOR. Likewise if pointing at a BEGIN statement, ↑N would move to the statement following the block, i.e. after the END statement. If the cursor is inside a block, or otherwise nested statement, then "↑" (this is the character "↑"—not the control key) will move the cursor up to the parent statement. Finally, an "@" will move the cursor to the statement that will be executed next by the interpreter. That is, if the program had been running and had returned control to the editor after hitting a breakpoint, then "@" would move the cursor to the statement where the breakpoint was.

To insert a new statement or clause into the program at the current cursor location one types ↑I, or equivalently ⟨tab⟩. The editor will insert a blank line in the program and allow the user to enter the statement using the line editor. After the line has been entered the editor will parse it in the current context of the program and report any syntax errors. The editor tries to be somewhat intelligent here and will fill in any unspecified fields. Certain keywords may be omitted, such as the DO in WHILE and FOR loops. The editor will only insert complete statements, so when the user enters the first line of a complex statement, the editor will also insert any other parts of the statement that are needed to complete it. For example, when a BEGIN is entered the corresponding END is automatically added. If the user typed only the keyword WHILE then the editor would also insert a null condition, the following keyword DO, and an empty statement as the body of the loop.

These added fields can later be modified by the user to whatever is desired. In this way the program being edited is always kept in a syntactically correct form.

Some structure editors never allow the user to enter a keyword, e.g. the Cornell Program Synthesizer [Teitelbaum 1981]. Instead they have the user insert a given template which has all the keywords already present. These templates are specified by a special command usually consisting of some (hopefully) mnemonic abbreviation. While this may work for a subset of common computer programming languages, when the number of possible language constructs increases, the number of these abbreviations becomes unwieldly. For example, the number of template specifiers used by the Cornell Program Synthesizer is around twenty. For AL, with all of its various motion statements and clauses, over three times that number would be needed.

If an undeclared variable is referenced in the inserted text, the editor will try to deduce its datatype and insert a declaration statement for it in the program. These declarations are inserted in the outermost block of the program or current procedure (if any).

The editor is designed to insert one new statement/clause per line, but it does allow the user to insert multiple statements, separated by semicolons, on the same line. There is currently no special insert mode for typing in several new lines; each line must be preceded by ↑I or ⟨tab⟩. However, collect mode, described below with the debugger commands, provides a way to enter a number of statements.

To modify a line of the program the user types a ⟨space⟩ which will load the current line into the line editor and open it for changes. The modified line will be parsed to make sure that it agrees with the syntax of the language. As with insertions, if an undeclared variable is referenced, a new declaration statement will be inserted to declare the variable. In keeping with the idea of maintaining the program's integrity, only those parts of the line that can be changed are modifiable with the line editor; it becomes more of an expression editor, operating on the expressions between keywords. So if the editor is pointing at an IF statement, only the expression between the IF and the THEN can be modified.[1] A major disadvantage of this, common to all "structure editors", is that it is very difficult, if not impossible, to transform a statement into another type, e.g. a FOR loop into a WHILE loop.

Whenever a new variable is declared either by the insertion of a new declaration statement or the modification of an old one, the block containing that declaration is reparsed to reflect any changes made by the introduction of the new or modified variable. Reparsing also occurs when a variable declaration is deleted.

Statements can be deleted with ↑D. Note this deletes the entire statement, so if the cursor was at an IF statement, the entire IF statement, including both the THEN and ELSE clauses, would be deleted. If pointing to a clause of a statement, then only that clause is deleted. With the cursor at the ELSE clause of an IF statement only the ELSE clause would be deleted, and the IF and THEN parts would remain unchanged. Also, since only complete statements are allowed, if, for example, the body of a WHILE loop was deleted, it would be replaced by an empty statement. If a numeric argument is given the delete command, then that number of statements or clauses at the current level will be deleted. If the number requested is greater than the number of statements or clauses at the current level, then only they are deleted; delete will not move up to a higher level.

Similar to the delete command are the commands to attach, ↑A, and copy, ↑C statements and clauses. The indicated lines of text are placed in a special attach buffer. The first and last few lines of which are highlighted on the display. The normal cursor motion commands are used to move the attached lines around in the program. When the place to deposit them is reached, the command ↑E will re-insert them into the program at the current cursor location, if this is syntactically possible. If it is not, then an error message will be printed, and the attached lines will remain attached. When the attach buffer is successfully inserted into the program, it is reparsed to assure that all variable references are bound correctly. Neither attach nor copy has yet been implemented in the current version of the AL system.

Using the extended MARK command one can mark up to twenty lines in the program. The ↑G command will move to the next mark in the program. ↑\-↑G will move to the previous mark. A mark may be cleared by moving the cursor to it and issuing the UNMARK command. To clear all of the current marks at once, one types "UNMARK ALL".

The ↑G command can also be used to move the cursor to a procedure or label by typing the procedure or label name terminated by a ↑G. This has not yet been implemented in the current system though.

A special command "[" exists to surround (bracket) a statement with a BEGIN-END block. This is useful, for example, if initially the body of a WHILE loop contained a single statement and the user now wishes to add another statement to it.

While not yet implemented, ↑F is reserved for use as a search command. The token to search for is entered through the line editor after the ↑F. A related extended command to rename a variable is "RENAME ⟨old name⟩⟨new name⟩" which searches for the innermost block, surrounding the current cursor position, which defines a variable ⟨old name⟩ and changes its name to ⟨new name⟩, updating all of the old references to it. RENAME has also not yet been implemented.

Finally, "?" or the extended HELP command will provide the user with access to on-line help. When it is implemented this will consist of the user typing keywords to select entries from various menus to move about in a tree of nodes, each of which displays appropriate information.

Line Editor

As mentioned above, a special line editor is used for entering extended commands, inserting new lines, or modifying old ones. As the user types characters, they are added to the current line. At any time, the user can move the cursor within the line to correct any mistakes that may have been made. When the user has finished editing the line, it is then passed back to the regular editor for processing.

The basic line editor commands include several to reposition the cursor. ↑A advances it one character to the right while ⟨bs⟩ moves it back one character. ↑F and ↑E move it to the front or end of the line, respectively. ↑S will search to the right for the next character typed, and if one is found in the current line, the cursor will be repositioned at it. ↑B is similar, but searches back to the left.

↑D will delete the character to the right of the cursor. At the end of the line, or when in insert mode, ⟨bs⟩ will delete the character to the left of the cursor. ↑K is like ↑S, but will kill all the characters between the current cursor position and the searched for character. ↑L kills to the left. ↑R will repeat the last search or kill command. The entire line can be cleared (zeroed) with ↑Z, while ↑O will restore the line to its initial (old) condition.

Most of the above commands can also take a numeric argument, like the basic editor commands, which is indicated by typing a ↑\ followed by the number.

When a regular (non-control) character is typed it will overwrite whatever character the cursor had been pointing to, unless the cursor was at the end of the line, in which case the new character is added to the line. In either case the cursor is then advanced to the next character. ↑I causes the line editor to enter insert mode whereupon subsequently typed regular characters will be inserted to the left of the cursor. In insert mode ⟨bs⟩ is a deleting backspace. Typing any control character will cause the line editor to leave insert mode. ↑T will transpose the two characters to the left of the cursor.

Any control character not mentioned above will cause the line editor to exit and pass back the line in its final form. Several of these have a special effect when editing the program (as opposed to entering an extended editing command). The normal terminating character is ⟨cr⟩, though any unmentioned control character acts similarly, which will have the editor move the cursor to the following line. ↑U will move it up one line. ↑N and ↑P respectively cause the next or previous line to be opened for modification, i.e. it is loaded into the line editor.

Editing Examples

Some examples of the editor in operation will now be shown. First is the creation of a trivial program to print out the numbers 1 through 10, along with their squares. Initially the editor looks like this:

```
***** Line    1 *********************
  BEGIN
> END
***** Cursor at Line   2 of   2 *****
  Welcome to AL
```

where ``>'' is used to denote the cursor's position. An introductory message is displayed in the echo window. Now after the user types ↑I in preparation for inserting a FOR statement, the display looks like:

```
***** Line    1 **********************
  BEGIN
>_
  END
***** Cursor at Line    2 of    3 *****
Welcome to AL
↑I
```

A new line has been inserted at the cursor line and the line editor positioned there. " __ "is the cursor. When the user enters the keyword FOR, the display becomes:

```
***** Line    1 **********************
  BEGIN
>FOR_
  END
***** Cursor at Line    2 of    3 *****
Welcome to AL
↑I
```

The user can now type a carriage return to have a template of the FOR statement inserted, or can proceed to explicitly enter the fields. Assuming a ⟨cr⟩ is typed, the display will look like:

```
***** Line    1 **********************
  BEGIN
  FOR 0 := 0 STEP 0 UNTIL 0 DO
>    /* statement */;
  END
***** Cursor at Line    3 of    4 *****
Welcome to AL
↑I OK
```

Note the empty statement created for the body of the FOR loop. If the user now wishes to fix up the fields of the FOR statement, the cursor would be moved back to it with a backspace, ⟨bs⟩, and the statement opened for modification by typing a space. At this point the display looks like:

```
***** Line    1 **********************
  BEGIN
> FOR 0 := 0 STEP 0 UNTIL 0 DO
    /* statement */;
  END
***** Cursor at Line    2 of    4 *****
Welcome to AL
↑I OK ↑H OK
```

Note that ⟨bs⟩ is printed as ↑H. Using the line editor, assume the user fills in the fields yielding the following display:

```
***** Line    1 *********************
  BEGIN
> FOR i := 1 STEP 1 UNTIL 10_ DO
    /* statement */;
  END
***** Cursor at Line    2 of    4 *****
Welcome to AL
↑I OK ↑H OK
```

After typing a ⟨cr⟩ to exit from the line editor, the editor proper notes that the variable "i" has not been defined. A message stating that an undeclared identifier was encountered is printed and a declaration statement for it inserted yielding:

```
***** Line    1 *********************
  BEGIN
  SCALAR i;
  FOR i := 1 STEP 1 UNTIL 10 DO
>   /* statement */;
  END
***** Cursor at Line    4 of    5 *****
↑I OK ↑H OK
UNDECLARED VARIABLE - WILL TRY TO DEFINE IT
OK
```

Now the user can insert a PRINT statement by typing a ↑I followed by

print(i, i↑2)

Unless explicitly stated, all entered lines, like the above, are terminated with a return. This completes the program, and running it would yield:

```
***** Line    1 *********************
  BEGIN
  SCALAR i;
  FOR i := 1 STEP 1 UNTIL 10 DO
    PRINT(i, i ↑ 2);
> END
***** Cursor at Line    5 of    5 *****
  OK ↑I OK
run
1 1 2 4 3 9 4 16 5 25 6 36 7 49 8 64 9 81 10 100
ALL DONE  OK
```

At this point the user might notice that all the numbers are printed on the same line. So the cursor might be moved back to the PRINT statement, a space typed to open it, followed by a ↑E to move to the end of the print list, the string "crlf" inserted, and finally a ⟨cr⟩ yielding:

```
***** Line    1 *********************
  BEGIN
  SCALAR i;
  FOR i := 1 STEP 1 UNTIL 10 DO
    PRINT(i, i ↑ 2, CRLF);
> END
***** Cursor at Line    5 of    5 *****
run
1 1 2 4 3 9 4 16 5 25 6 36 7 49 8 64 9 81 10 100
ALL DONE  OK ↑H OK    OK
```

Running the program again would have the numbers printed one pair per line.

A second example describes creating a slightly more realistic program. It has the green arm[2] move in a circular motion, approximated by a regular polygon of n sides, of radius r, parallel to the table and about the point $(x,y,5)$. The program will request that the parameters, n, r, x, and y be typed in by the user at execution time.

Again the initial display consists of a single BEGIN-END pair. As a first step, variables for the needed parameters are declared by typing ↑I followed by

```
scalar n,r,x,y
```

At this point the display looks like:

```
***** Line   1 **********************
  BEGIN
  SCALAR n, r, x, y;
> END
  ***** Cursor at Line   3 of   3 *****
  ↑I
  NEED TO REPARSE...
  OK
```

Whenever a new variable is added to the program, the editor needs to reparse the enclosing block to maintain proper lexical scoping. In this case there is nothing to reparse. Next, the user inserts two statements that will prompt for the number of points to use in approximating the circle. Before typing the ⟨cr⟩ to pass the line to the editor the display looks like:

```
***** Line   1 **********************
  BEGIN
  SCALAR n, r, x, y;
>print("How many points to use? ")  n := inscalar_
  END
  ***** Cursor at Line   3 of   4 *****
  ↑I
  NEED TO REPARSE...
  OK ↑I
```

After the ⟨cr⟩ is typed the two statements are parsed. Note that in this case the ";" between the two statements will be automatically supplied by the editor. After inserting the two statements, the editor's prettyprinter displays them one per line:

```
***** Line   1 **********************
  BEGIN
  SCALAR n, r, x, y;
  PRINT("How many points to use? ");
  n := INSCALAR;
> END
  ***** Cursor at Line   5 of   5 *****
  ↑I
  NEED TO REPARSE...
  OK ↑I OK
```

In a like manner other statements are added to read in values for r, x, and y yielding:

```
***** Line   1 *********************
BEGIN
SCALAR n, r, x, y;
PRINT("How many points to use? ");
n := INSCALAR;
PRINT("Radius? ");
r := INSCALAR;
PRINT("Center? (X,Y) ");
x := INSCALAR;
y := INSCALAR;
> END
***** Cursor at Line  10 of  10 *****
↑I
NEED TO REPARSE...
OK ↑I OK ↑I OK ↑I OK
```

Next, the frame used to specify the position of the center of the circle is defined by inserting an assignment statement. Note that it has not been declared yet, and the editor must insert a declaration for it.

```
***** Line   1 *********************
BEGIN
FRAME centre;
SCALAR n, r, x, y;
PRINT("How many points to use? ");
n := INSCALAR;
PRINT("Radius? ");
r := INSCALAR;
PRINT("Center? (X,Y) ");
x := INSCALAR;
y := INSCALAR;
centre := FRAME(NILROT,VECTOR(x,y,5)*INCHES);
> END
***** Cursor at Line  12 of  12 *****
OK ↑I OK ↑I OK ↑I OK ↑I
UNDECLARED VARIABLE - WILL TRY TO DEFINE IT
OK
```

Likewise, assignment statements defining a frame to specify the position of a point located on the circumference of the circle of radius r, and a rotation to twist the point $1/n$ of the way around the circle are inserted and declarations for them added by the editor. For the purposes of this example the window size is fifteen lines. The newly inserted statements cause the program to be larger than the window, and so the top line is now off the screen. Note the change in the upper border line.

```
..... Line   2 .....................
FRAME pt;
ROT twist;
FRAME centre;
SCALAR n, r, x, y;
PRINT("How many points to use? ");
n := INSCALAR;
PRINT("Radius? ");
r := INSCALAR;
PRINT("Center? (X,Y) ");
x := INSCALAR;
y := INSCALAR;
centre := FRAME(NILROT,VECTOR(x,y,5)*INCHES);
twist := ROT(ZHAT,360 / i * DEGREES);
pt := FRAME(ROT(YHAT,180*DEGREES),r * XHAT * INCHES);
> END
***** Cursor at Line  16 of  16 *****
OK ↑I
UNDECLARED VARIABLE - WILL TRY TO DEFINE IT
OK
```

Note that while the position of the center of the circle is expressed in world coordinates,[3] the point, *pt*, on the circumference is expressed with respect to the coordinate system defined by *centre*. The multiplication *centre∗pt* will express the location of this point in world coordinates, which is necessary if the manipulator is to be moved there. Also note that the orientation of *centre*, specified by the predeclared system constant NILROT, is the same as that of the world coordinate system: the z axis points straight up, and the x and y axes are aligned along the sides of the table the manipulators are mounted on. The orientation of *pt* has the z axis pointing downwards, which is how the manipulator will need to be oriented when traversing the circle.

Now the loop to move around the circle is inserted by typing the line

for i: =0 til n

This causes yet another variable to be declared. Also, "til" is a predeclared macro which is expanded by the editor. The display now looks like:

```
..... Line   5 .....................
FRAME centre;
SCALAR n, r, x, y;
PRINT("How many points to use? ");
n := INSCALAR;
PRINT("Radius? ");
r := INSCALAR;
PRINT("Center? (X,Y) ");
x := INSCALAR;
y := INSCALAR;
centre := FRAME(NILROT,VECTOR(x,y,5)*INCHES);
```

```
   twist := ROT(ZHAT,360 / i * DEGREES);
   pt := FRAME(ROT(YHAT,180*DEGREES),r * XHAT * INCHES);
   FOR i := 0 STEP 1 UNTIL n DO
>     /* statement */;
   END
***** Cursor at Line  18 of  19 *****
OK ↑I
UNDECLARED VARIABLE - WILL TRY TO DEFINE IT
OK
```

The body of the loop will take several statements so a BEGIN-END block is inserted by typing ↑I followed by

  begin

The corresponding END statement is automatically inserted by the editor. The display is now:

```
..... Line   6 .....................
   SCALAR n, r, x, y;
   PRINT("How many points to use? ");
   n := INSCALAR;
   PRINT("Radius? ");
   r := INSCALAR;
   PRINT("Center? (X,Y) ");
   x := INSCALAR;
   y := INSCALAR;
   centre := FRAME(NILROT,VECTOR(x,y,5)*INCHES);
   twist := ROT(ZHAT,360 / i * DEGREES);
   pt := FRAME(ROT(YHAT,180*DEGREES),r * XHAT * INCHES);
   FOR i := 0 STEP 1 UNTIL n DO
      BEGIN
>     END;
   END
***** Cursor at Line  19 of  20 *****
OK ↑I
UNDECLARED VARIABLE - WILL TRY TO DEFINE IT
OK ↑I OK
```

Finally, statements to move the arm to the next point on the circle and to then compute the following point are inserted. The cursor is then advanced past the END statement of the FOR loop by typing a ⟨cr⟩, and a final statement to park the arm is added. The final display for this program is then:

```
..... Line   9 .....................
   PRINT("Radius? ");
   r := INSCALAR;
   PRINT("Center? (X,Y) ");
   x := INSCALAR;
   y := INSCALAR;
   centre := FRAME(NILROT,VECTOR(x,y,5)*INCHES);
   twist := ROT(ZHAT,360 / i * DEGREES);
   pt := FRAME(ROT(YHAT,180*DEGREES),r * XHAT * INCHES);
```

```
    FOR i := 0 STEP 1 UNTIL n DO
    BEGIN
    MOVE GARM TO centre * pt;
    pt := twist * pt;
    END;
  MOVE garm TO gpark;
> END
  ***** Cursor at Line  23 of  23 *****
  UNDECLARED VARIABLE - WILL TRY TO DEFINE IT
  OK ↑I OK ↑I OK ↑I OK
  OK ↑I OK
```

At this point, if the user wished to modify the FOR statement the cursor could be moved to it by, for example, a series of 6 ⟨bs⟩'s, a "<" and 2 ⟨bs⟩'s, or ↑\-2↑N. The last way says to move up two statements, staying at the current lexical level. The command ↑\-2↑S would move up two statements to the END statement of the FOR loop. From there, or anywhere else in the body of that block, typing "↑" would move the cursor to the BEGIN statement in the FOR loop. Another "↑" would move to the block's parent statement, in this case the FOR statement. Yet another "↑" would move to the outermost block of the program, the parent block of the FOR statement.

Several further examples are given in the next section after the various debugging commands are described. The examples will show how the editor is used to lend special support to creating manipulator programs.

3.3 Debugger

In addition to being used to modify AL programs the editor is also used as the interface between the user and the AL interpreter. It is through the debugging facilities of the editor that the user can run his or her program, try out various statements, examine and modify variable values, set and clear breakpoints, etc. As mentioned earlier, all terminal input and output done by a running AL program appears in the editor's echo window. The commands available to run and debug AL programs are described below.

When a new program is read in with the GET command, any old user variables are eliminated and the variables in the outermost block of the new program are created. As the user modifies the program, the runtime environment is also modified to reflect the addition of new variables or the deletion of old ones.

Debugging Commands

To run the AL program currently being edited, one uses the RUN command (START is equivalent). Control is then passed to the AL interpreter which will run the program, commencing execution with its first statement. Control will stay with the interpreter until either (1) the program finishes, (2) an ABORT statement is executed, (3) a breakpoint is encountered, or (4) the user types ↑C. After one of the above has occurred, the user will again be in communication with the editor/debugger. The editor will then move the cursor to the statement the interpreter was about to execute next. The "@" command will subsequently return the cursor to this statement. A program which has been interrupted may be resumed with the PRO-CEED command. Control is passed back to the interpreter and execution will continue from where it left off.

The user can use the TRACE command to show the names of any active procedures in the current process, along with the line number of their currently executing statement. Since AL does support parallel process, TRACE ALL will show all of the currently active processes and tell what state they are in.

In addition to specific debugging commands, the user can also evaluate expressions and type in AL statements for immediate execution. Any expressions or statements typed in are parsed in the context defined by the current cursor location. For global variables this does not matter much, but if, for example, procedure *A* calls procedure *B*, which then breaks to the debugger, then to examine any variables local to procedure *A* the user must first move the cursor to the body of procedure *A*. An example of this which further discusses using the editor to set the current context is given below. Expressions are evaluated and their values are printed out. Currently only one expression per line is allowed.

Any valid AL statement may be entered for immediate execution. Statements may extend over several lines. While the statement is being entered the user is talking to the parser which will prompt for another line with an "*". In general, statements must be terminated with a ";". Once the statement is read in, a new process is created to execute it. Any old processes will be suspended until the new one has finished. This new process may in turn be interrupted by a breakpoint, and suspended while a newer process is initiated and run. The outermost of these processes may be flushed with the POP command.

In addition to immediately executing statements from the debugger, it is also possible to have them inserted into the user's AL program and then executed. This is done by enabling "collect" mode with the command SET COLLECT ON. This can later be turned off by SET COLLECT OFF. When collecting is enabled, any statements typed in for immediate execution will be automatically inserted into the program at the current cursor location and then executed.

A statement in the current program may be immediately executed with the EXECUTE command. Whatever statement the cursor is pointing to will be executed.

The DEFINE command will create and insert into the program an assignment statement that assigns a variable a constant whose value is equal to the variable's current value as specified by the interpreter. The keyword DEFINE is followed by a list of the variables the user wishes to have defined.

When the cursor is pointing to an AFFIX statement, the AT command will compute the spatial relationship between the two affixed frames, using their current values. This value will then be used to update the AT phrase of the affixment statement.

The user can set a breakpoint at a statement with the BREAK command. This can later be removed with the UNBREAK command. All the breakpoints may be cleared at once by typing "UNBREAK ALL". Up to twenty-five breakpoints may be set at any one time.

In addition to explicitly placing breakpoints, the user can step through the program in several ways. The STEP command places temporary breakpoints at all statements the current statement can pass control to, including procedure and function calls. The interpreter will break back to the editor when it hits one of these. All temporary breakpoints are then cleared. The SSTEP command is similar to STEP, except that it treats procedure and function calls as atomic and does not insert breakpoints in them. The NSTEP command is like SSTEP, but only inserts breakpoints at the same lexical level, i.e. it will not descend into block structure. The GSTEP command takes a giant step up to the lexical level of the current statement's parent. SSTEP, NSTEP and GSTEP can be thought of as analogous to the editor commands ↑S, ↑N, and "↑" (actually "↑" followed by ↑N). Finally, there is the TSTEP command which will set a temporary breakpoint at the cursor's current location and transfer control to the interpreter as if a PROCEED command had been given.

If more than one process is active, then the process currently pointed to by the editor is the one that will be single stepped. As the editor is positioned in the program it maintains a pointer to the process associated with the statement the cursor is pointing to. The various flavors of STEP commands then use the statement this process is about to execute when setting the temporary breakpoints. The process also determines the environment used when evaluating expressions.

Rather than continuing program execution from wherever it had stopped, the user can have execution commence from the current cursor location with the GO command.[4] When there are multiple processes the GO command is more complicated. The process currently pointed to by the editor is the one whose control flow is altered. In addition when control is passed to the interpreter it is this process that will be run first, even if some other process had been running when execution had been interrupted. Any environments associated with active blocks at a greater lexical depth than that of the statement being jumped to are flushed. Also flushed are any processes that were sprouted by a coblock, which is no longer active, or by a procedure call, along with any of their descendants.

For some of the more commonly used commands given above, abbreviated versions exist. Typing "!" to the editor tells it that a debugger command follows. These debugger commands are: !R for RUN, !P for PROCEED, !X for EXECUTE, !S for STEP, !A for SSTEP (since procedure calls are atomic), !N for NSTEP, !G for GSTEP, !T for TSTEP, and !B for BREAK/UNBREAK. For !B what happens depends on the preceding numeric argument, if any (i.e. "↑\<arg>!B"). It will be BREAK if ⟨arg⟩ is positive, UNBREAK if ⟨arg⟩ is negative, and UN-BREAK ALL if ⟨arg⟩ is zero.

There is a special mode to facilitate debugging of parallel processes. In it all WAIT statements are turned into PROMPT's and all SIGNAL statements into

PRINT's. Thus it is possible to run and debug a single thread of a COBEGIN block. If the user jumps into a COBEGIN block, via the GO command, this mode is automatically enabled. The command SET NOWAIT ON manually enables it, while SET NOWAIT OFF disables it. Alternatively, one can use SET WAIT OFF/ON. An example of this will be shown later. For the SET command if neither ON nor OFF is specified, ON will be assumed.

While the program is running, any input or output will appear in the echo window. For this reason if the program does much i/o it makes sense to use a large echo window size. (C.f. SET BOTSIZE ⟨n⟩ command in previous section.) When the user's program is awaiting input the normal line editor is not used. Since only single characters and numbers are being entered all that is provided is a deleting ⟨bs⟩.

Example Program Development Sessions

This section will show several example sessions of using the AL editor and debugger to develop various manipulator programs. The first of these is an example of the classic pick and place problem: an object is sitting at point *A* and needs to be moved to point *B*. Initially the editor contains a "null" program consisting of a single BEGIN-END block. Before starting, the echo window size is increased from 3 to 5 with:

```
set botsize 5
```

Again, unless explicitly stated, all lines entered are terminated with a return. The first step is to move the arm to the object. In this case the user does this by releasing the brakes for the Stanford blue arm and moving it there manually. This could also be done by typing in explicit motion statements. Now, to make the position slightly more accurate, the user types:

```
center barm;
```

to have the system close the blue arm's fingers on the object, and in doing so shift the arm so it is centered over the object. The center command is passed directly to the interpreter for immediate execution. It is not added to the program being written. At this point the display looks like:

```
***** Line   1 *********************
  BEGIN
> END
***** Cursor at Line   2 of   2 *****
set botsize 5
  OK
center barm;
  OK
```

The current position of the blue arm can be determined by typing in the expression

pos(barm)

which will cause the display to look like:

```
***** Line    1 *********************
  BEGIN
> END
***** Cursor at Line    2 of    2 *****
center barm;
  OK
pos(barm)
VECTOR( 4.21, 40.03, 1.87)
  OK
```

Next, a frame variable, *pickup*, to hold the value of the object's initial location is assigned the current value of the arm with

pickup := barm;

This statement is also executed immediately, but a declaration statement for the frame is added to the program. At this point the display looks like:

```
***** Line    1 *********************
  BEGIN
  FRAME pickup;
> END
***** Cursor at Line    3 of    3 *****
  OK
pickup := barm;
UNDECLARED VARIABLE - WILL TRY TO DEFINE IT
        ↑
  OK
```

The "↑" shows where in the statement the undeclared variable was detected. At this point the user can have the system type out the value of *pickup* by entering the expression

pickup

causing the display to look like:

```
***** Line    1 *********************
  BEGIN
  FRAME pickup;
> END
***** Cursor at Line    3 of    3 *****
        ↑
  OK
pickup
TRANS(ROT(VECTOR(0.1,0.99,0.04),178),VECTOR(4.21,40.03,1.87))
  OK
```

Note that the arm is not pointing quite straight down. This is a common result when it is moved by hand rather than under computer control. Using the DEFINE extended command an assignment statement for *pickup* using its current value can be inserted.

```
***** Line   1 **********************
BEGIN
FRAME pickup;
pickup := TRANS(ROT(VECTOR(0.1,0.99,0.04),178*DEGREES),
                    VECTOR(4.21,40.03,1.87)*INCHES);
> END
***** Cursor at Line   4 of   4 *****
pickup
TRANS(ROT(VECTOR(0.1,0.99,0.04),178),VECTOR(4.21,40.03,1.87))
OK
define pickup
OK
```

At this point the user might back the cursor up and modify the value so the orientation of *pickup* is pointing straight down. Afterwards the display appears:

```
***** Line   1 **********************
BEGIN
FRAME pickup;
pickup := TRANS(ROT(YHAT,180*DEG),VECTOR(4.2,40,1.85)*INCHES);
> END
***** Cursor at Line   4 of   4 *****
TRANS(ROT(VECTOR(0.1,0.99,0.04),178),VECTOR(4.21,40.03,1.87))
OK
define pickup
OK ↑H OK
OK
```

After correcting the statement in the program that will define an initial value for the variable *pickup*, the user will probably wish to also update the current value of the variable kept by the system. A simple way to do this is to back up and execute the newly modified statement.

```
***** Line   1 **********************
BEGIN
FRAME pickup;
> pickup := TRANS(ROT(YHAT,180*DEG),VECTOR(4.2,40,1.85)*INCHES);
END
***** Cursor at Line   3 of   4 *****
execute
OK
pickup
TRANS(ROT(VECTOR(0,1,0),180),VECTOR(4.2,40,1.85))
OK
```

Next, the user will probably want to reposition the arm so it has the correct orientation. To do this, commands must be entered to open the fingers, move to the pickup location, and, finally, use center to regrasp the object. These are the same instructions that the user will want in the program to initially grasp the object, so before entering them, collect mode is turned on and the cursor positioned where the statements should be inserted. Midway through the sequence the display looks like:

```
***** Line   1 *********************
BEGIN
FRAME pickup;
pickup := TRANS(ROT(YHAT,180*DEG),VECTOR(4.2,40,1.85)*INCHES);
OPEN bhand TO 3.5 * INCHES;
> END
***** Cursor at Line   5 of   5 *****
OK
set collect on
OK
open bhand to 3.5 * inches;
OK
```

and after the other two commands have been entered:

```
***** Line   1 *********************
BEGIN
FRAME pickup;
pickup := TRANS(ROT(YHAT,180*DEG),VECTOR(4.2,40,1.85)*INCHES);
OPEN bhand TO 3.5 * INCHES;
MOVE barm TO pickup;
CENTER barm;
> END
***** Cursor at Line   7 of   7 *****
OK
move barm to pickup;
OK
center barm;
OK
```

Having defined the pickup location and the instructions necessary to grasp the object, the next step is to repeat the above process for the destination position. Before doing so, collect mode is disabled, so any instructions entered for immediate execution are not added to the program. After having successfully defined the destination location the display appears as:

```
***** Line   1 *********************
BEGIN
FRAME setdown;
FRAME pickup;
pickup := TRANS(ROT(YHAT,180*DEG),VECTOR(4.2,40,1.85)*INCHES);
setdown := TRANS(ROT(YHAT,180*DEG),VECTOR(15,44,1.85)*INCHES);
> OPEN bhand TO 3.5 * INCHES;
MOVE barm TO pickup;
```

```
CENTER barm;
END
***** Cursor at Line   6 of   9 *****
setdown := barm;
UNDECLARED VARIABLE - WILL TRY TO DEFINE IT
        ↑
 OK
define setdown
 OK ↑H OK   OK
```

Having defined the set down position the user would now use the editor to insert the motion statement to move the object from the initial to the final position. Then statements to release the object and move the arm away would also be inserted. After this has been done the program looks like:

```
***** Line   1 **********************
BEGIN
FRAME setdown;
FRAME pickup;
pickup := TRANS(ROT(YHAT,180*DEG),VECTOR(4.2,40,1.85)*INCHES);
setdown := TRANS(ROT(YHAT,180*DEG),VECTOR(15,44,1.85)*INCHES);
OPEN bhand TO 3.5 * INCHES;
MOVE barm TO pickup;
CENTER barm;
MOVE barm TO setdown;
OPEN bhand TO 3.5 * INCHES;
MOVE barm TO bpark;
> END
***** Cursor at Line   12 of   12 *****
define setdown
 OK ↑H OK   OK
 OK
 OK
 OK ↑I OK ↑I OK ↑I OK
```

This is the simplest AL program to do the pick and place operation and before adding any refinements the user will probably want to try it out with the RUN command. Afterwards the user saves a copy of the program in the file TRY1.AL. The display now is:

```
***** Line   1 **********************
BEGIN
FRAME setdown;
FRAME pickup;
pickup := TRANS(ROT(YHAT,180*DEG),VECTOR(4.2,40,1.85)*INCHES);
setdown := TRANS(ROT(YHAT,180*DEG),VECTOR(15,44,1.85)*INCHES);
OPEN bhand TO 3.5 * INCHES;
MOVE barm TO pickup;
CENTER barm;
MOVE barm TO setdown;
OPEN bhand TO 3.5 * INCHES;
MOVE barm TO bpark;
> END
***** Cursor at Line   12 of   12 *****
 OK ↑I OK ↑I OK ↑I OK
run
ALL DONE  OK
save try1.al
 OK
```

Note that when the program finishes execution the cursor is moved to the final END statement. While running the above program if the user had not placed an object at the pickup location, then the centering operation would have reported an error and prompted the user for what to do next. If the user requests control be passed back to the debugger the display would look like:

```
***** Line   1 *********************
BEGIN
FRAME setdown;
FRAME pickup;
pickup  := TRANS(ROT(YHAT,180*DEG),VECTOR(4.2,40,1.85)*INCHES);
setdown := TRANS(ROT(YHAT,180*DEG),VECTOR(15,44,1.85)*INCHES);
OPEN bhand TO 3.5 * INCHES;
MOVE barm TO pickup;
> CENTER barm;
MOVE barm TO setdown;
OPEN bhand TO 3.5 * INCHES;
MOVE barm TO bpark;
END
***** Cursor at Line   8 of   12 *****
run
BARM - EXCESSIVE FORCE ENCOUNTERED      JOINT(S) =  7
"P" TO PROCEED, "R" TO RETRY THE MOTION
OR "B" TO BREAK TO DEBUGGER: b
OK
```

At this point note that the cursor has been set to the statement where the error occurred. Typing "PROCEED" now would cause the CENTER statement to be retried. To recover from the error the user needs to open the fingers of the hand and then place the object where it was supposed to have been. Then the CENTER can be done correctly, and the rest of the program executed:

```
***** Line   1 *********************
BEGIN
FRAME setdown;
FRAME pickup;
pickup  := TRANS(ROT(YHAT,180*DEG),VECTOR(4.2,40,1.85)*INCHES);
setdown := TRANS(ROT(YHAT,180*DEG),VECTOR(15,44,1.85)*INCHES);
OPEN bhand TO 3.5 * INCHES;
MOVE barm TO pickup;
CENTER barm;
MOVE barm TO setdown;
OPEN bhand TO 3.5 * INCHES;
MOVE barm TO bpark;
> END
***** Cursor at Line  12 of   12 *****
OK
open bhand to 3.5;
OK
proceed
ALL DONE   OK
```

This concludes the pick and place example. The next example will show the use of the various single stepping commands. A simple small program to print some numbers is used for the example. Initially the display is:

```
***** Line   1 *********************
> BEGIN
  SCALAR i, j;
  j := 0;
  PRINT("Starting - ");
  FOR i := 1 STEP 1 UNTIL 5 DO
    BEGIN
    j := j + i;
    PRINT(i);
    END;
  PRINT(" = ",j);
  END
***** Cursor at Line  1 of  11 *****
get sdemo.al
NO ERRORS DETECTED
  OK
```

Running the program produces:

```
***** Line   1 *********************
  BEGIN
  SCALAR i, j;
  j := 0;
  PRINT("Starting - ");
  FOR i := 1 STEP 1 UNTIL 5 DO
    BEGIN
    j := j + i;
    PRINT(i);
    END;
  PRINT(" = ",j);
> END
***** Cursor at Line  11 of  11 *****
NO ERRORS DETECTED
  OK
run
Starting - 1 2 3 4 5 =  15
ALL DONE  OK
```

If the cursor is backed up to the PRINT statement inside of the loop and a TSTEP command issued to proceed until reaching the current cursor position then:

```
***** Line   1 *********************
  BEGIN
  SCALAR i, j;
  j := 0;
  PRINT("Starting - ");
  FOR i := 1 STEP 1 UNTIL 5 DO
    BEGIN
    j := j + i;
>   PRINT(i);
    END;
```

```
PRINT(" = ",j);
END
***** Cursor at Line   8 of  11 *****
ALL DONE   OK ↑H OK ↑H OK ↑H OK
tstep
BPT   OK
i
 1
OK
```

To confirm where the interpreter is in the loop, the user has it type out the current value of the loop variable *i*, which is 1 since this is the first time through the loop. At this point the user has several choices of single stepping available. STEP, SSTEP, and NSTEP would all advance execution to the END statement on line 9. The GSTEP command, which the user actually enters, takes a giant step up to the parent statement of the PRINT, which is the BEGIN block:

```
***** Line    1 *********************
    BEGIN
    SCALAR i, j;
    j := 0;
    PRINT("Starting - ");
    FOR i := 1 STEP 1 UNTIL 5 DO
>     BEGIN
      j := j + i;
      PRINT(i);
      END;
    PRINT(" = ",j);
    END
***** Cursor at Line   6 of  11 *****
gstep
 1
BPT   OK
i
 2
OK
```

The "1" in the echo window following the GSTEP command is from the PRINT statement in the loop which was just executed. Now both STEP and SSTEP would break at the assignment to *j*. The NSTEP command, which is entered, causes the program to continue until the next statement at the same lexical level of the BEGIN is encountered. In this case, that will be when the BEGIN is again encountered the next time around the loop. The NSTEP command causes all of the statements inside the block to be executed. So the display is now:

```
***** Line    1 *********************
    BEGIN
    SCALAR i, j;
    j := 0;
    PRINT("Starting - ");
    FOR i := 1 STEP 1 UNTIL 5 DO
>     BEGIN
      j := j + i;
      PRINT(i);
```

```
      END;
    PRINT(" = ",j);
    END
  ***** Cursor at Line   6 of   11 *****
  nstep
    2
  BPT   OK
  i
    3
  OK
```

Another GSTEP command will move back up to the lexical level of the block's parent statement, the FOR statement, before breaking to the debugger. This means that the interpreter will break when it gets to the PRINT statement following the FOR loop. Thus:

```
  ***** Line    1 *********************
  BEGIN
  SCALAR i, j;
  j := 0;
  PRINT("Starting - ");
  FOR i := 1 STEP 1 UNTIL 5 DO
    BEGIN
    j := j + i;
    PRINT(i);
    END;
> PRINT(" = ",j);
  END
  ***** Cursor at Line   10 of   11 *****
  gstep
   3 4 5
  BPT   OK
  i
    6
  OK
```

A more realistic example will now be shown that consists of the user trying to debug one motion sequence in a larger assembly. The motion being debugged is to put a nut that the fingers are holding into a socket driver which is mounted in place. The problem is that the arm is not accurate enough to just directly place the nut in the socket driver, so a strategy involving both force sensing and active compliance will be used. The first step is to move the nut down until it makes contact with the top of the socket. In doing this a deliberate offset is introduced so the nut is known to be on one side of the socket. Then it is moved across the center of the socket, with the arm exerting a downward pressure to push the nut in, while also being compliant to translational forces arising from contact with the sides of the socket opening [Mujtaba 1982].

Initially the display is:

```
  ..... Line 101 ....................
  { Move to above driver, with an offset! }
> MOVE barm TO nut_drop + 0.3 * YHAT * INCHES
    VIA nut_drop + 2 * ZHAT * INCHES
```

```
WITH SPEED_ FACTOR = 2
ON FORCE >= 10 * OZ ALONG ZHAT DO
    STOP BARM;
{ Now move it over until it goes in }
MOVE barm TO nut_drop - 2 * ZHAT * INCHES
    WITH STIFFNESS = (20,30,10,100,200,100)
    WITH FORCE = 40 * OZ ALONG ZHAT
    WITH SPEED_ FACTOR = 3;
{ Now release nut and get stem to attach to it }
OPEN bhand TO 1.5 * INCHES;
MOVE barm TO # + 0.5 * ZHAT;
..... Cursor at Line 102 of 207 .....
OK
```

Since the user expects to need to run this code a number of times to make it work reliably, a mark is put at the first motion statement involved, and a breakpoint set after the second motion. Thus it will only take one command, a ↑G, to reposition the editor's cursor at the beginning of the sequence, and the interpreter will return control to the user when it has finished executing the sequence. This is done by issuing a MARK command while the cursor is at the first motion statement, then moving with ↑S's down to the comment statement before the next operation starts, and setting a breakpoint with BREAK. The display is now:

```
..... Line 101 .....................
{ Move to above driver, with an offset! }
MOVE barm TO nut_drop + 0.3 * YHAT * INCHES
    VIA nut_drop + 2 * ZHAT * INCHES
    WITH SPEED_ FACTOR = 2
    ON FORCE >= 10 * OZ ALONG ZHAT DO
        STOP BARM;
{ Now move it over until it goes in }
MOVE barm TO nut_drop - 2 * ZHAT * INCHES
    WITH STIFFNESS = (20,30,10,100,200,100)
    WITH FORCE = 40 * OZ ALONG ZHAT
    WITH SPEED_ FACTOR = 3;
>  { Now release nut and get stem to attach to it }
   OPEN bhand TO 1.5 * INCHES;
   MOVE barm TO # + 0.5 * ZHAT;
   ..... Cursor at Line 112 of 207 .....
   OK
mark
   OK ↑S OK ↑S OK ↑S OK
break
   OK
```

Now the user can try out the two motions by first moving to the mark with ↑G and invoking the interpreter by typing "GO." The arm will then move down until it makes contact with the driver, and then slide over to, hopefully, place the nut in the socket. Actually, the user notices that when the arm slides over, it does not move in a straight line. This is because the trajectory is computed in joint space, and not Cartesian space.[5] To rectify this, the user inserts several VIA points in the sliding motion. Another problem the user observed, again during the sliding motion, was that the arm was pushing down with too much force. So the bias force specified should be decreased. After all of this, the display looks like:

```
..... Line 101 .....................
{ Move to above driver, with an offset! }
MOVE barm TO nut_drop + 0.3 * YHAT * INCHES
   VIA nut_drop + 2 * ZHAT * INCHES
   WITH SPEED_ FACTOR = 2
   ON FORCE >= 10 * OZ ALONG ZHAT DO
      STOP BARM;
{ Now move it over until it goes in }
MOVE barm TO nut_drop - 2 * ZHAT * INCHES
   VIA nut_drop + vector(0.0,0.5,-1.0) * INCHES
   VIA nut_drop + vector(0.0,0.0,-1.0) * INCHES
   VIA nut_drop + vector(0.0,-0.5,-1.0) * INCHES
   WITH STIFFNESS = (20,30,10,100,200,100)
   WITH FORCE = 25 * OZ ALONG ZHAT
>  WITH SPEED_ FACTOR = 3;
{ Now release nut and get stem to attach to it }
..... Cursor at Line 114 of 207 .....
OK ↑G OK
go
BPT   OK ↑H OK ↑H OK ↑H OK ↑I OK ↑I OK ↑I OK
OK    OK
```

After making the above modifications to the program the user is ready to try it again to see if it now works. First, though, the arm needs to be repositioned above the socket driver. So, the user enters a MOVE statement for immediate execution to do so, and then retires the nut insertion. Note that "#" means use the arm's current position.

```
..... Line 101 .....................
{ Move to above driver, with an offset! }
MOVE barm TO nut_drop + 0.3 * YHAT * INCHES
   VIA nut_drop + 2 * ZHAT * INCHES
   WITH SPEED_ FACTOR = 2
   ON FORCE >= 10 * OZ ALONG ZHAT DO
      STOP BARM;
{ Now move it over until it goes in }
MOVE barm TO nut_drop - 2 * ZHAT * INCHES
   VIA nut_drop + vector(0.0,0.5,-1.0) * INCHES
   VIA nut_drop + vector(0.0,0.0,-1.0) * INCHES
   VIA nut_drop + vector(0.0,-0.5,-1.0) * INCHES
   WITH STIFFNESS = (20,30,10,100,200,100)
   WITH FORCE = 25 * OZ ALONG ZHAT
   WITH SPEED_ FACTOR = 3;
> { Now release nut and get stem to attach to it }
..... Cursor at Line 115 of 207 .....
OK    OK
move barm to # + 3*zhat;
OK ↑G OK
go
BPT   OK
```

This time the insertion works perfectly. To assure reliability the user is apt to try the code a number of times more before moving on to debug the next part of the program.

The next example will be shown to discuss the use of the editor in defining the debugging context. The program being debugged involves a call from the main program to a procedure. After the program is started the display looks like:

```
***** Line    1 *********************
 BEGIN
 SCALAR i, j;
 PROCEDURE foo;
   BEGIN
   SCALAR i;
   i := 99;
   ABORT("In procedure foo");
>  PRINT("In foo i = ",i,CRLF);
   END ;
 i := 1;
 j := 2;
 foo;
 PRINT("In main i = ",i);
 END
***** Cursor at Line   8 of  14 *****
 run
 In procedure foo
 ABORTING
 OK
 trace
 (ACTIVE) RUNNING foo: 8    (MAIN)/12
 OK
```

The TRACE command shows the currently active call sequence. The program is currently stopped at line 8 while in procedure *foo*, which was called from line 12 of the main program. Now the main program and the procedure both define a scalar variable called *i*. If the user types in an expression involving it then the variable used will depend on the cursor's position. If the cursor is pointing to a statement in the body of the procedure then the variable defined in the procedure is used. If the cursor is outside of the procedure then the global variable named *i* will be used. For example:

```
***** Line    1 *********************
 BEGIN
 SCALAR i, j;
 PROCEDURE foo;
   BEGIN
   SCALAR i;
   i := 99;
   ABORT("In procedure foo");
>  PRINT("In foo i = ",i,CRLF);
   END ;
 i := 1;
 j := 2;
 foo;
 PRINT("In main i = ",i);
 END
***** Cursor at Line   8 of  14 *****
 OK
 i
 99
 OK
 i + j
 101
 OK
```

Note that the global variable *j* is accessible from the procedure. If the cursor is moved out of the procedure and the same two expressions requested then:

```
***** Line   1 *********************
BEGIN
SCALAR i, j;
PROCEDURE foo;
  BEGIN
  SCALAR i;
  i := 99;
  ABORT("In procedure foo");
  PRINT("In foo i = ",i,CRLF);
  END ;
  i := 1;
  j := 2;
> foo;
  PRINT("In main i = ",i);
  END
***** Cursor at Line  12 of  14 *****
OK > OK
i
1
OK
i + j
3
OK
```

If a TRACE command is done now, it will show the status of the currently selected context, not where execution was interrupted.

```
***** Line   1 *********************
BEGIN
SCALAR i, j;
PROCEDURE foo;
  BEGIN
  SCALAR i;
  i := 99;
  ABORT("In procedure foo");
  PRINT("In foo i = ",i,CRLF);
  END ;
  i := 1;
  j := 2;
> foo;
  PRINT("In main i = ",i);
  END
***** Cursor at Line  12 of  14 *****
3
OK
trace
(MAIN)/11
OK
trace all
PROCESS 1 (ACTIVE) RUNNING foo: 8   (MAIN)/12
OK
```

Proceeding will continue from where execution was suspended, independent of whatever context is selected using the editor. However, if the user changes the execution flow with a GO command then it is the current editing context that determines which process is affected. Finally, note that typing a "@" will move the cursor back to where execution was suspended, and in doing so restore the original context.

For this example, the system is just moving up the call chain of the single active process. In other cases, there are apt to be several processes active, each with its own call chain. An example involving multiple processes will be shown next.

This last example shows a program that uses multiple processes to control two arms in a cooperative task. The red arm first goes and grabs an object, then moves it to where the green arm can reach it. The green arm then moves over to the object, takes it from the red arm, and moves it to its final destination. This is essentially the same as the pick and place example above, except that it takes two arms to perform the operation, and the motions of the two arms must be coordinated so they do not get in each other's way or drop the object being passed. There are three synchronization points in the program: when the red arm has moved the object to the passing point, when the green arm has grabbed it, and when the red arm has released it. To coordinate the motions of the arms, three events are used to signal when these synchronization points are reached. A separate process is associated with each arm. An AL program for this is shown below:

```
BEGIN
{Program to pass an object from one arm to the other}
EVENT passed, caught, ready;
FRAME beam, pass, catch, pallet;
PROCEDURE passer;
  BEGIN "red"
  MOVE RARM TO beam;
  CENTER RARM;
  MOVE RARM TO pass;
  PRINT("ready -- ");
  SIGNAL ready;
  WAIT caught;
  OPEN RHAND TO 3 * INCHES;
  PRINT("released -- ");
  SIGNAL passed;
  END "red";
PROCEDURE catcher;
  BEGIN "green"
  OPEN GHAND TO 3 * INCHES;
  WAIT ready;
  MOVE GARM TO catch;
  CENTER GARM;
  PRINT("got it!",CRLF);
  SIGNAL caught;
  WAIT passed;
  MOVE GARM TO pallet;
  PRINT("passed!",CRLF);
  END "green";
```

```
beam   := FRAME(ROT(YHAT,180*DEG),VECTOR(40,25,3)*INCHES);
pass   := FRAME(ROT(YHAT,180*DEG),VECTOR(42,30,12)*INCHES);
catch  := FRAME(ROT(YHAT,180*DEG),VECTOR(42,37,12)*INCHES);
pallet := FRAME(ROT(YHAT,180*DEG),VECTOR(37,40,3)*INCHES);
COBEGIN
 passer;
 catcher;
COEND;
END
```

It should be mentioned that, in this simple example of two-arm control, only one arm is ever in motion at a time. Because of this it would be easy to write a program that did not use multiple processes and, hence, had no need to signal or wait for events. However, in other assemblies the two arms might be working fairly independently of each other, and only loosely coupled when, for example, one might pass a completed sub-assembly to the other.

If the user reads in this program, sets a temporary breakpoint after the first WAIT statement in the catcher procedure, and then starts it running, the display will appear:

```
..... Line  12 ......................
    WAIT caught;
    OPEN RHAND TO 3 * INCHES;
    PRINT("released -- ");
    SIGNAL passed;
    END "red";
  PROCEDURE catcher;
    BEGIN "green"
    OPEN GHAND TO 3 * INCHES;
    WAIT ready;
>   MOVE GARM TO catch;
    CENTER GARM;
    PRINT("got it!",CRLF);
    SIGNAL caught;
    WAIT passed;
    MOVE GARM TO pallet;
    PRINT("passed!",CRLF);
    END "green";
..... Cursor at Line  21 of  37 .....
 OK > OK ↑N OK > OK !T
ready --
BPT  OK
trace all
PROCESS 1 PROCESS JOIN WAIT (MAIN)/33
PROCESS 2 EVENT WAIT passer: 13   (MAIN)/34
PROCESS 3 (ACTIVE) RUNNING catcher: 21   (MAIN)/35
 OK
```

Note the use of the abbreviated form of the TSTEP command: "!T." At this point the main process has sprouted two sub-processes in the coblock on line 33, and it is currently waiting for them to finish. The first of these has called the passer procedure, and is waiting for the catcher procedure to grab the object. The other has called the catcher procedure which has hit the temporary breakpoint placed there by the user. If the user were to now request the debugger to single STEP, the MOVE statement at line 21 would be executed and the interpreter would hit a breakpoint at the CENTER statement which follows on line 22. If, however, the cursor were moved to any statement in the passer procedure, and a STEP command issued, then the breakpoint would be set for the next statement in passer. The interpreter would resume execution of catcher, performing the CENTER, PRINT, SIGNAL and WAIT statements (lines 22–25), at which point the process would block, and the passer process resume. The interpreter would then immediately hit the breakpoint set by STEP, and break to the debugger. The display would then look like:

```
     ..... Line  12 .....................
       WAIT caught;
  >    OPEN RHAND TO 3 * INCHES;
       PRINT("released -- ");
       SIGNAL passed;
       END "red";
     PROCEDURE catcher;
       BEGIN "green"
       OPEN GHAND TO 3 * INCHES;
       WAIT ready;
       MOVE GARM TO catch;
       CENTER GARM;
       PRINT("got it!",CRLF);
       SIGNAL caught;
       WAIT passed;
       MOVE GARM TO pallet;
       PRINT("passed!",CRLF);
       END "green";
     ..... Cursor at Line  13 of  37 .....
     OK < OK < OK !S
    got it!
    BPT  OK
    trace all
    PROCESS 1 PROCESS JOIN WAIT (MAIN)/33
    PROCESS 2 (ACTIVE) RUNNING passer: 13   (MAIN)/34
    PROCESS 3 EVENT WAIT catcher: 26   (MAIN)/35
     OK
```

Thus, the user can step through one process while the others are running normally. In the event of an error in one process, the user can manually enter immediate statements to recover, and then back up that process with the GO command. This allows one process to be reset, without having to disturb the others.

This program will be used to show another feature of the system concerned with debugging multiple processes. Before running the program, the user is apt to want to try each procedure by itself. However, the user cannot just type in a procedure call to *catcher* for immediate execution. If that were done, then after opening the green hand the interpreter would hang waiting for the event ready to be signalled. The user could regain control by interrupting the interpreter with a ↑C, then manually signal the event and proceed, but this is awkward. Since this is a fairly common situation in debugging coordinated multiple processes, a special "nowait" mode exists. Once in nowait mode, the interpreter turns all WAIT statements into PROMPT's and all SIGNAL statements into PRINT's. The user can instruct the system to enter nowait mode by typing

```
set nowait on
```

The display after running *catcher* while in nowait mode would look like:

```
..... Line  15 ......................
  SIGNAL passed;
  END "red";
PROCEDURE catcher;
  BEGIN "green"
  OPEN GHAND TO 3 * INCHES;
  WAIT ready;
  MOVE GARM TO catch;
  CENTER GARM;
  PRINT("got it!",CRLF);
  SIGNAL caught;
  WAIT passed;
  MOVE GARM TO pallet;
  PRINT("passed!",CRLF);
  END "green";
  beam := FRAME(ROT(YHAT,180 * DEGREES),VECTOR(40,25,3) * INCHES);
..... Cursor at Line  13 of  37 .....
set nowait on
 OK
catcher
WOULD WAIT FOR EVENT: ready
TYPE P TO PROCEED: p
got it!
WOULD SIGNAL EVENT: caught
WOULD WAIT FOR EVENT: passed
TYPE P TO PROCEED: p
passed!
 OK
```

Nowait mode is useful for two different reasons. As shown by the example above, it allows part of one process to be run without the need to also have any other processes that it is coupled with running simultaneously. It is also useful to show the user exactly what state the world is in when the process encounters a WAIT statement.

If the user's program has a deadlock in it—that is, two processes waiting on each other—then when it is run and that part of the program is reached the system will just sit there, doing nothing. The user can force control back to the debugger with a ↑C, and use the TRACE ALL command to discover the deadlock. The program can be edited to correct the problem and then continued after the user manually signals one, or both, of the deadlocking events.

3.4 Interpreter

When an AL program is ready for execution, control is passed to the interpreter. The interpreter executes the statements in the user's AL program, interacts with the arm servo process to move the manipulators, and finally returns control back to the user. The user interacts with the interpreter primarily through the debugger commands discussed in the previous section.

While the program is running, any input or output will appear in the echo window. Since the only input to the interpreter consists of single characters and numbers, the normal line editor is currently not used (primarily due to space considerations). All that is provided is a deleting ⟨bs⟩.

As was mentioned in the previous section, the interpreter continues running until either: (1) the program finishes, (2) an ABORT statement is executed, (3) a breakpoint is encountered, or (4) the user types ↑C. Control is then returned to the editor/debugger.

Since AL supports parallel execution of statements the interpreter handles multiple processes and schedules them. The interpreter's scheduling algorithm is to run the highest priority process until either it terminates or blocks, or a higher priority process becomes active. A process can block by initiating a motion, requesting input from the terminal, waiting for an event to be signalled, going to sleep, etc. When a blocked process once again becomes ready to run, it is added to the end of the list of active processes. Thus when a COBEGIN block is entered, the first statement will be run until it blocks, then the second until it blocks, then the third, and so on until the last statement is started. Then any of the previous statements that had blocked and are now ready to proceed will be continued.

Condition monitors are run at a priority one greater than that of the process that defines them. The main program runs at a priority of zero. Any condition monitors it spawns run at a priority of one. If any of those condition monitors define other condition monitors, they will be run at a priority of two, and so on. There are four basic types of condition monitors currently allowed by AL. Event, duration, and force sensing condition monitors are respectively triggered when the event they are waiting on is signalled, the time interval has elapsed, or the arm servo process signals that the specified force threshold has been crossed. Expression condition monitors are treated somewhat differently. The expression they trigger on is evaluated periodically (currently every 100 milliseconds), and if it is true then the condition monitor's body will be executed. The reason for periodic evaluation of the expression is because this type of condition monitor is primarily envisioned to monitor expressions involving devices, which are continuously changing their values. Eventually the interpreter will also immediately reevaluate the expression whenever a variable in it is updated. Moreover, it will distinguish between those expressions that involve devices, directly or indirectly, and hence need to be periodically evaluated, and those which do not.

3.5   Force Graphics System

Part of the old AL system is the GAL module which has been developed for graphing data collected during motions of the arms. The force components to be examined are specified by means of a GATHER clause associated with the MOVE statement for the motion in question. The user can display the gathered force data in a number of different ways. This feedback concerning the forces occurring during the motion greatly facilitates the debugging of motions and force strategies.

At the moment these force graphing capabilities have not been incorporated into the new interactive AL system. This section will describe the old GAL subsystem that was a module in the previous compiler-based AL system. At the end of the section there will be a brief discussion of how force graphing may be added to the new AL system.

Force Graphics System Commands

The old AL runtime system runs on the PDP-11/45, which is interfaced to the various manipulator arms and devices. The runtime system and the user's AL program are down loaded into the PDP-11/45 from a program running on the DEC KL10, the two machines being connected by a special interface. The GAL graphics module is run on the DEC KL10 in parallel to the runtime system, communicating with it over this interface. When a force gathering motion has completed, the runtime system passes the information collected over to GAL, which then allows the user to display it on the terminal's screen.

When run, GAL responds with: "AL Force Data Gathering Module" and prompts with an asterisk for the user's command. Commands consist of one or two characters. The possible commands the user can give to GAL fall into two distinct classes. The first of these are the system-related commands dealing with down loading a new AL program, reloading the runtime system, and interrupting the runtime system to transfer control to the debugger on the PDP-11/45. These are described in the AL user's manual [Goldman and Mujtaba 1981] and will not be dealt with here other than to note that they provided a clean interface between the user and the AL system. Prior to GAL, the down-loading process required the user to know a certain amount about various system utility programs that had nothing to do with AL. GAL eliminated the need for these programs by the average user, and, in fact, became the preferred method of running AL programs, even if no force displaying was to be done.

The other class of GAL commands is related to the graphic display of the collected force information. These commands fall into four categories: what to display, how to display it, whether to save it, and how to coordinate activities with the AL runtime system.

To have a force component displayed, the user types FX, FY or FZ to display force data along the specified axis, MX, MY or MZ to display torque data about the specified axis, and T1, T2, T3, T4, T5, or T6 to display torque data about the specified joint.

For each force graph, the vertical axis represents the gathered force or torque value. Forces are measured in ounces, and torques in ounce-inches. The horizontal axis represents the time from the beginning of the motion. It is marked off not by seconds, but by samples, 60 of which are taken each second. To show how the force behaves just after the arm has stopped being servoed, but while it is still settling, the runtime system continues to gather force data for the next half second. These last thirty samples are distinguished from the others by a dashed vertical line indicating where the servoing ended.

The force is graphed according to two parameters that the user can set. The first of these selects between continuous and discrete graphing. For continuous graphs the line representing the force values is linearly interpolated between sample points. Sometimes it is necessary, though, to see the force data as the arm servo sees it—discretely, with no interpolation between samples.[6] The graph mode select command toggles between these two ways of presenting the data. Example force graphs are shown below, one graphed continuously, the other discretely.

The other parameter that the user can set deals with the scaling of the vertical axis. The axis can be automatically scaled so that it matches the range of the col-

Figure 3.1.   Continuous Force Graph

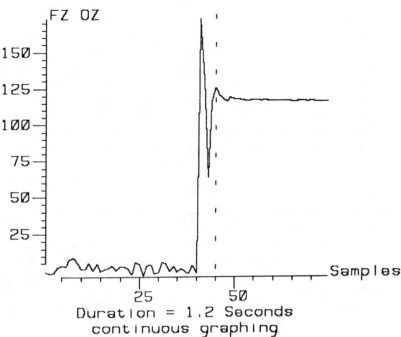

Figure 3.2.   Discrete Force Graph

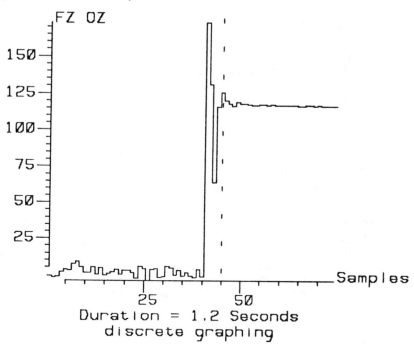

lected data, or the scaling factor can be fixed independent of the data's range. When the user selects the automatic scaling mode, the system guarantees that all of the data points will fit in the graph. This is usually what the user wants, but sometimes the user will wish to see the smaller valued forces in greater detail, or, more frequently, will wish to compare the force graphs for different components. In these cases the fixed scaling mode is selected. The user can double or halve the fixed scaling factor to suit the range of the data. Some sample force graphs below will show the same data graphed with both automatic and fixed scaling.

Note the difficulty of comparing the two components when the scaling is done automatically. Contrast this with the same data displayed with fixed scaling.

Now, it can more easily be seen that one of the graphs shows a greater maximum force at the peak, and that the force after the arm settles is the same for both.

GAL will only display one force graph on the screen at a time; ideally, several graphs should be displayed simultaneously to facilitate comparisons amongst them. Fortunately, the time taken by GAL to shift from the display of one collected component to another is quite small, so the user can flip back and forth quickly and make the necessary observations to compare them.

A hardcopy plot of the currently displayed force graph can be made. To do this, the user specifies a file to store the plot in, along with a title for it. Later,

Figure 3.3. Automatic Scaling

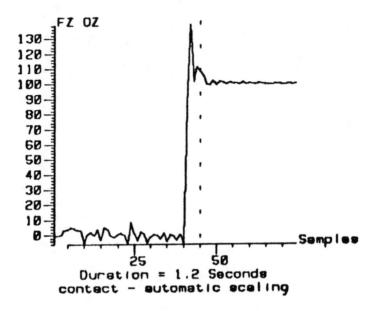

Duration = 1.2 Seconds
contact - automatic scaling

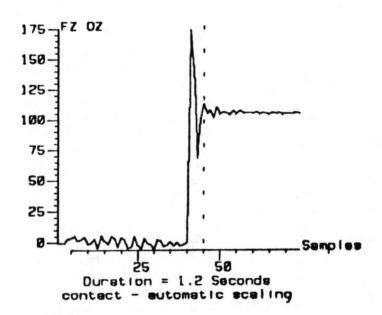

Duration = 1.2 Seconds
contact - automatic scaling

Figure 3.4. Fixed Scaling

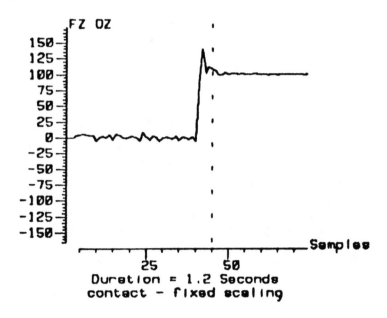

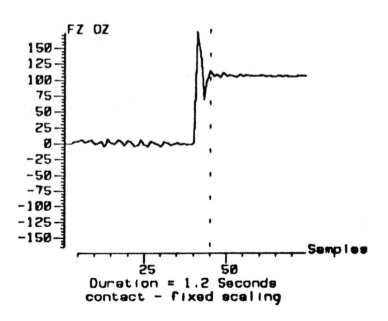

another program, PLOT, can be run to read in the file, re-display the force graph, and write out a copy to the XGP (Xerox Graphics Printer).

The final category of graphic commands coordinates the interaction between GAL and the AL runtime system. Usually after a gathering motion is completed, the user will wish to examine the force data before the AL program continues with the next motion. In particular, it is not a good idea for the arm to commence a motion while the user's attention is elsewhere, in this case on the displayed force graphs. Also, since GAL only maintains the data collected from the last gathering motion, if the program proceeded with another one, then the old force data would be overwritten with the new values, possibly before the user had finished examining them. To deal with these concerns there are three different modes of interlocking GAL with arm motions. The default mode is to have the AL runtime system pause when it reaches the next motion statement in the user's AL program. To proceed the user must issue an explicit GAL command. The next mode of operation is for the AL program to continue running until the next gathering motion is reached. The runtime system will then pause until told to continue by GAL. The third and final mode is one where the runtime system never pauses between any motions. This is useful when running a program containing many gathering motions that the user wishes to run until a given condition occurs, and then examine the data collected during the last gathering motion.

Example Force Graphs

Several example force graphs will now be shown along with the AL statements that generated them. All of the examples are taken from a program that assembled lawn sprinklers. In particular the examples focus on the steps required to insert the sprinkler stem into the body. Below is a drawing of the sprinkler stem and body.

The insertion operation commences with the sprinkler stem located a few inches above the hole in the sprinkler body. The axes of the stem and of the hole are roughly parallel. The positional accuracy of the arm is not sufficient to directly insert the stem into the hole in the body, so a strategy using force sensing and compliance is required to find the hole. Then the stem can be inserted using force compliance.

The first step of the insertion operation is to move the sprinkler stem down until it makes contact with the body in the well near the hole. To do this a motion statement is used to move the stem down until a threshold is exceeded for the force along the axis of motion.

```
{ Find bottom of sprinkler well }
MOVE barm TO stem_ touch * down2
  WITH DURATION = 2 * SECONDS
  WITH GATHER = (FZ)
  ON |FORCE| >= 5 * OZ ALONG ZHAT DO
    STOP barm;
```

Figure 3.5. Sprinkler Stem and Body

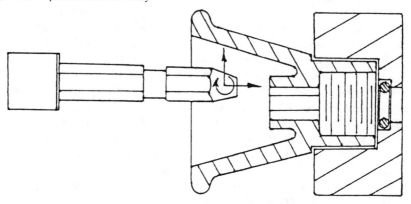

When the above statement is executed a force graph like the one below is generated.

Figure 3.6. Contact Force

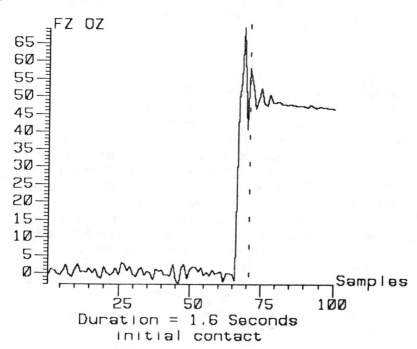

This graph is very similar to other graphs of contact forces. For example, compare it to the other force graphs given above which also show contact forces. Note the characteristic way in which the force rapidly builds up, and how it rings a bit at the end as the arm settles. Even though the condition monitor was set to terminate the motion when the force exceeded 5 ounces, due to the speed the arm was moving, the force built up to much more than this before the arm servo responded and the motion was halted.[7] If delicate parts were being used the force graph clearly indicates that a slower arm motion is called for to avoid damaging them. Finally, note the noise in the signal that is present before contact is made. It is important that the specified threshold level be sufficiently above the noise level.

Next, the hole in the body must be located and the tip of the stem placed in it. This is accomplished by moving the stem tip back and forth in the well while pushing down on it. The arm's stiffness has been specified such that, when it passes over the hole, it will catch and stay in the hole.

```
{ Find hole by wiggling stem back and forth }
MOVE barm TO loc * down1
    VIA loc * down1, loc * upright, loc, loc * upleft, loc, loc * rot20
    VIA loc, loc * downright, loc, loc * downleft, loc * rotm20, loc
    WITH DURATION = 3 * SECONDS
    WITH FORCE_ WRIST NOT ZEROED
    WITH STIFFNESS = (30,30,0,200,500,200) ABOUT stem_ tip
    WITH TORQUE = 10 * OZ * INCHES ABOUT ZHAT
    WITH FORCE = pressing_ force * OZ ALONG ZHAT
    WITH GATHER = (MX,MY,FZ,FX,FY);
```

A typical force graph for this step is shown below. It shows the forces encountered while pushing down on the sprinkler stem. Note how complicated this graph is compared to the others. The manipulator is attempting to exert a downwards bias force of 25 ounces, which is shown by the first two peaks. As the stem tip slides over the central well of the sprinkler body, it will drop to follow the contour of the well, reducing the downwards pressure. The pressure will also drop when the tip enters the hole, which happened about two thirds of the way through the motion in this case. Finally, at the end the forces build up as the manipulator tries to move the stem further into the hole, and the stem subsequently jams.

This is the least reliable step in the insertion operation, and so it is important to be able to test whether the hole finding operation was successful. A simple check based on a force exceeding a given threshold will not work here due to the compliant nature of the motion. To determine whether the manipulator has succeeded or not, the distance moved along the stem's axis is measured. This distance will be very slight unless the stem tip enters the hole, so by testing whether it is above a given threshold the program can decide whether the operation needs to be retried. The hole can usually be found given several tries.

Figure 3.7.   Finding the Hole

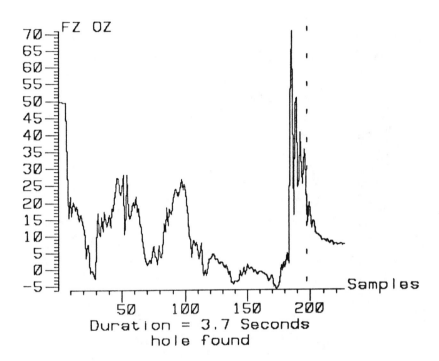

The final step is to push the stem down into the body. The fixture holding the body also holds a rubber o-ring which will fit onto the notched region of the stem and keep it from slipping out of the hole. To avoid jamming while seating the stem, the arm twists it back and forth a bit while pushing downwards. The stiffness of the arm is also set to make it somewhat compliant. Note that the chosen center of compliance is at the stem tip which makes the motion as though the stem were being pulled, rather than pushed, into the hole.

```
{ Push stem into o-ring.}
MOVE BARM TO loc * down2
   VIA loc * TRANS(ROT(ZHAT,-30 * DEGREES), ZHAT * inch)
   VIA loc * TRANS(ROT(ZHAT,30 * DEGREES), 2 * ZHAT * INCH)
   WITH FORCE_ WRIST NOT ZEROED
   WITH STIFFNESS = (30,30,50,50,40,40) ABOUT STEM_ TIP
   WITH FORCE(ZHAT) = inserting_ force * OZ
   WITH GATHER = (FZ,FX,FY,MZ)
   ON |FORCE(ZHAT)| >= 80 DO STOP BARM
   WITH DURATION = 2.5 * SECONDS;
```

The force graph for this final insertion is shown below.

Figure 3.8.   Final Insertion

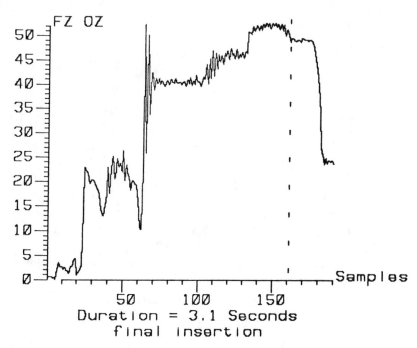

A number of interesting facts can be observed in the graph. First, note that initially the arm moves smoothly downwards, but then catches, causing the force to build up. When the force reaches a certain point the stem slips free and moves further into the hole. Again it catches, and again, it slips free when the force builds up sufficiently. The force then builds up as the stem is inserted into the o-ring, but that it stays at about 20 ounces, which was the value of the variable *inserting_force*. Almost immediately after the o-ring slips into place the fingers of the hand holding the stem bump into the sprinkler body resulting in the characteristic contact force shape. The contact force is less than the threshold specified in the condition monitor, so the motion is not terminated here as it should be. By examining the graph, a more reasonable threshold value can be determined, and the user can modify the above statement for subsequent insertions.

Finally, the force gradually builds up as the arm servo attempts to move the arm further down along the nominal trajectory. Because the arm cannot physically move down any further this results in the "spring" along the axis of motion being stretched, and the force increases accordingly.

The above final insertion operation is quite robust, and once the hole is found it is virtually guaranteed that the stem will be properly seated in the hole. Occasionally, however, the stem will jam when being inserted into the hole.[8] The graph below shows the forces that occurred when the stem jammed. Note how the force smoothly builds up after the part jams.

Figure 3.9. Jamming During the Insertion

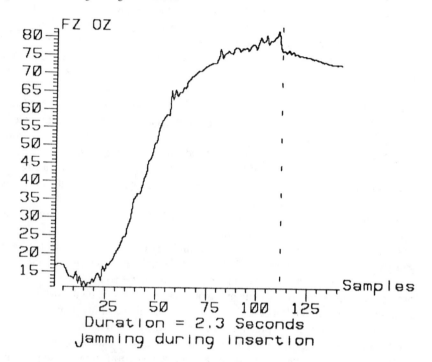

Jamming during insertion

Working with force graphs has greatly aided debugging assembly operations involving force and compliance. Having a force graph to look at allows the user to see whether the program's force strategy is being successful or not. The user can watch as forces cyclically build up and then drop when the frictional force is overcome. By being able to monitor sliding and contact friction, the user can attempt to reduce it via appropriate bias forces and arm stiffnesses. As mentioned in the final insertion example above, inspecting the force graph enables appropriate force thresholds to be set. Likewise, the user can observe noise during an operation and take it into account when setting force thresholds.

The use of force graphs also helps when doing research in force servoing. Being able to easily examine forces led to the current filtering used to monitor force thresholds. Identify characteristic force signatures, such as those shown by typical contact forces, is essential for extended force sensing abilities, and simplifying what the user needs to specify.

Incorporating Force Graphics in Interactive AL

When a force graphics capability is added to the new interactive AL system it will, of course, need to provide commands to select and display the various gathered force components. How these will differ from the old GAL subsystem will largely depend on what sort of graphics terminal is used and how it is connected to the computer running AL. The design of GAL was heavily influenced by the use of a separate computer system for it. In particular, a separate display terminal, complete with keyboard, was involved. Also, commands to GAL had to be entered through this other computer.

The commands used for force graphics displaying are ideally suited for menu selection by either a light pen, mouse, or similar device, should such hardware be available. Given a large, high resolution screen it would become feasible to display several force graphs simultaneously. This would facilitate making comparisons of different force components for one or several motions, which would be quite useful. Most likely, force graphs would be displayed on a separate screen and not on the same one used by the AL editor, though given a large enough screen this need not be the case.[9]

As mentioned above, there is a slight problem when the user's attention is split between two terminals. This manifests itself primarily with regard to the interlock mechanism used to stop future arm motions after force data has been gathered. At that point in the old GAL system the user must switch attention from one screen to the other. After examining the force data, a command to continue program execution is given and attention must again be focused on the main screen. A more flexible interlock mechanism should be possible with the new interactive AL system. When the interpreter is waiting for the force data to be examined it can break back to the editor/debugger as if a breakpoint had been encountered. After the user has examined the force data and is ready to continue, the program may be resumed with the PROCEED command.

Another addition that now becomes possible is to have the arm servo module always gathering data for all the force components for the last few seconds if no explicit GATHER clause is given. This unsolicited force data could then be examined on demand, for instance after a motion fails or a breakpoint is reached. Alternatively the force display module could be continuously displaying selected force components, automatically updating the display after each motion.

4

Implementation Details

This chapter goes into some of the details of the implementation of the AL system. It first discusses the way a program is internally represented. Then it proceeds to describe the insides of the various system modules: interpreter, editor, debugging facilities, and the force graphics subsystem, along with the other data structures used by them.

4.1 Overview

Before describing the details of the AL system, a short discussion of the surrounding environment is in order. First the hardware involved and then the software AL interacts with will be covered.

AL currently controls three different robot arms. These include an ancient Scheinman Stanford arm, known as the blue arm or barm, and two Unimate 600 Puma arms, referred to as the green and red arms, or garm and rarm. A force-sensing wrist is mounted on the blue arm, and new prototype force wrists are under development for the two pumas. Other devices available include an electric socket driver and a pneumatic vise.

Controlling all of these devices is a PDP-11/45 with 124 K words of memory, floating point hardware, various device related interfaces, a disk, and two terminals. The PDP-11/45 directly communicates with the joint microprocessors on the pumas through a standard DR11C interface. The RSX operating system is used on the PDP-11/45.

The AL system consists of two independent processes: the interpreter and user interface, which this book is all about, and the arm servo control process. The two processes interact by passing messages back and forth. For example, whenever the interpreter wants to move an arm it sends a message to the servo process, which will then initiate the motion and send a message back to the interpreter when it is completed. In the near future the arm servo process will be on a separate processor from the interpreter. Eventually we expect each arm will be servoed from its own dedicated processor(s).

The AL system is written almost entirely in Pascal. A few small modules that deal with message passing, terminal i/o, special operating system calls, etc. are written in assembly language. To run in the small memory address space available on the PDP-11/45, the interpreter process is heavily overlayed.

Two versions of the AL system currently exist. There is the version running under RSX on a PDP-11/45, which is described in this chapter, and there is another which runs on SAIL's KL10 under the WAITS operating system. The KL10-based version does not control any physical devices, but has been used to develop and test out the system.

4.2   Internal Program Representation

The current implementation of AL makes use of approximately twenty different record types to internally represent and interpret the user's AL program. Many of these, in turn, have numerous variant parts. In this section those record types used to store the user's AL program will be described. The others will be mentioned in the following sections when the module that uses them is discussed.

Internally the program is stored as a parse tree. The main nodes in the tree are statement records, one for each statement in the user's program. These statement nodes then point both to other statements and to expression subtrees. The following discussion will be somewhat bottom up to minimize the number of forward references.

Basic Data Types

At the bottom of things are the basic data types used by AL. Scalars are just the same as real numbers. Vectors consist of an array of three reals, one each for the X, Y and Z coordinate values. Transformations are stored in a 3 × 4 array of reals, the first three columns holding the rotation matrix and the last column holding the positional offset. Transformations are also used to hold rotations, the last column being all zeros then. Both vectors and transes also contain a reference count field. The reference count contains the number of places in the program that are making use of that vector or trans. When the count becomes zero the record will then be released. This reference count method is used instead of garbage collecting, which the previous implementation of AL used, to incur a uniform cost rather than having the system pause during execution at some random point in the program to garbage collect.

Strings consist of a list of records each containing an array of ten characters and a pointer to the next record in the string. The program node pointing at the string also contains a number telling how many characters are in the string. Strings are used for holding comments and identifiers. The only operation defined on strings in AL is assignment.

Variable Definition Records

Associated with each system and user defined variable is a variable definition record.

There are a number of fields that are common to each variable definition record, along with variants to hold the additional information needed for variables of specific data types. Each of these fields will be discussed in turn.

Each variable definition record points to an identifier record which in turn points to a string containing the name of the variable. More will be said about the identifier records when parsing is discussed later.

The base data type of the variable is contained in one field as a scalar type. Possible base types include both those explicitly declarable in an AL declaration statement: scalar, vector, rot, trans, frame, event, string and label, along with those implicit in other AL statements: condition monitor, dimension, macro and macro formal parameter, plus a special type for predeclared constants. Several bits in another field are used to indicate whether the variable is a procedure or an array or, if it is a parameter to some procedure, whether it is passed by reference or by value. Other bits are reserved for future use by the debugger—for example, to indicate that the interpreter should break back to the user when the variable is updated or referenced.

In AL each variable can have an associated physical dimension, such as time or distance. Therefore each variable definition has a pointer, to another variable definition record (described below), which defines the dimensionality.

Each variable has two numbers associated with it which are used by the interpreter to access that variable's value in the current environment. The first of these specifies the lexical level of the defining block, while the second gives the variable's offset in the block. More will be said about this in the next section when the interpreter is discussed.

The two final common variable definition record fields are used to make lists of variable definitions. All of the variables defined in a block are linked together on a single list for use by the interpreter. This list is used upon block entry and exit to respectively create and destroy the necessary variables used by the block. The variables in the list are ordered by their offset in the block. Those variables defined in each AL declaration statement are also linked together for use by the editor. Two lists are necessary since one represents the lexical structure of the program—that is, which variables make up a declaration statement—while the other reflects the temporal order in which the variables were defined. Initially these two orders are the same, but as the program is edited, and old variables destroyed and new ones created, they will diverge.

For the basic data types of scalar, vector, rot, trans, frame, event and string the above information is all that is needed to fully define the variable. The other variable types require one additional field. For labels this field is used to point to the statement that the label is associated with. For condition monitors there is a pointer to the statement that defines the condition monitor. Likewise for macro definitions. Macro formal parameters contain a pointer to the list of tokens currently bound to the formal while expanding the macro. Macros will be more fully discussed in the section relating to parsing.

Array variables contain a pointer to an array definition node, which specifies the number of dimensions in the array, points to the array bounds list, and has a flag used by the editor when printing out the array declaration that indicates if the array bounds are the same as the next array in the declaration statement, and hence need not be printed, e.g. "SCALAR ARRAY foo, bar[1:5]." Each node in the array bounds list contains two pointers to expression trees which are equivalent to the lower and upper bounds for that array index. There is also a third pointer to the next node in the array bounds list.

Procedures have a pointer to a procedure definition node. This node has a back pointer to the procedure's variable definition record. Another field points to a list of variable definition records which specify any formal parameters used by the procedure. A third field points to the statement composing the body of the procedure. For procedures that do not return any result the field in the procedure's variable definition record indicating the base data type is set to a special null type.

Variables that specify a dimension have a pointer to a dimension node. This node describes the physical dimensions of the variable in terms of time, distance, angle and force. Four integers are used to specify the exponents for these quantities. For example, acceleration would be specified by time having an exponent of –2, distance one of 1, and both angle and force set of 0. For torque the exponents would be 1 for both force and distance, and 0 for time and angle. Actually these integers are scaled by a factor of 64 to allow dimension checking to work when the expression being checked involves square root operations, causing the exponents to be divided by 2, rather than just being added or subtracted.

The final variable definition record variant is for predefined system constants. For these there is a pointer to a leaf node giving the value of the predefined constant.

Expression Nodes

Expressions are represented by trees consisting primarily of nodes for operators and leaves for constants and variables. The basic expression node consists of a field indicating the operation to be performed, three pointers for possible arguments of the operator, and an integer used by the editor to indicate the number of characters used to print out the expression. This last field is only set for the root expression node.

Leaf nodes come in several flavors, specified by a leaf type field. For variables the leaf node points to the variable's definition record. There is also a pointer to the identifier naming the variable. This second pointer is essential during the reparsing that occurs after an old variable has been deleted. More will be said about this in the section concerned with the editor.

For scalar constants, the leaf node contains the real number. It also contains a field used by the editor to indicate how many characters are required to print out the scalar's value. For vector and trans leaf nodes there is a pointer to the vector or trans value. For strings there is an integer giving the string's length, and a pointer to the record containing the first part of the string.

The final type of leaf node is for predefined system constants. It contains a back pointer to the constant's variable definition record, so the constant can be printed by name, rather than value, in expressions. It also contains a pointer to the leaf node holding the constant's value.

Both expression nodes and leaf nodes are variants of a very basic record type used for nodes at various places in the parse tree. This ubiquitous node record has over thirty variants used for expressions, motion statement clauses, and various flavors of lists. Node record variants that have been mentioned above include: list nodes, procedure definition nodes, array definition nodes, array bounds definition nodes, and physical dimension nodes. Whenever the word "node" is used when describing a record, it will almost invariably imply that a variant of the node record is involved. An exception to this is statement nodes in the parse tree that refer to statement records. The basic node record has a field specifying the node's type, and a pointer to another node record, used to create lists of nodes.

A bit more needs to be said about several types of expression nodes. Certain operators may have a variable number of arguments. These include the list of arguments passed in a procedure call, the indices of an array reference, and the print list associated with a query. In each of these cases the second argument of the expression node points to a list node. This list node has two pointers, one to the first expression in the list, and the second to another list node, which in turn contains a pointer to the next expression in the list. For procedure calls the first pointer of the expression node points to a variable leaf node which in turn points to the procedure's variable definition record. Likewise, for array references the first expression node pointer points through a variable leaf node to the array's variable definition record.

There is a special operator type used for bad expressions. When the parser cannot make sense out of part of an expression—for example, if it is the wrong data type to be the operand of some operator—it creates an expression node of type "bad." The first pointer field of the expression node points to the bad expression subtree, so it can be used for later editing, while the second pointer is used to point to a leaf node containing a zero default value of the proper data type. This keeps the interpreter from dying when it later tries to evaluate the expression.

Finally, in addition to the tree structure representation used for expressions there is also an evaluation ordering. Before interpreting a program the editor performs a preorder walk of the expression tree and, while doing so, sets up back pointers so the interpreter can later non-recursively traverse the tree in postorder. Thus during program execution the interpreter iterates down a list of expression nodes, and at each node the expression's operands are either constants, or precomputed and available on the stack. All of the expressions associated with a statement are so threaded, and the pointer to the resulting list is stored in the statement.

Statement Records

As mentioned earlier, each statement in the user's AL program has a statement record associated with it. Statements at the same lexical level are connected by doubly linked lists. The forward links are essential for interpreting the program. Both direction links are used by the editor to move about in the program and when inserting new statements or deleting old ones. The back pointer of the first statement in the list points back to the parent statement. The last statement in each list is always an END or COEND statement which also contains a back pointer to the parent statement of the list.

Each statement record has a pointer to the label attached to that statement, if any. This pointer is to the label's variable definition record, which in turn has its own pointer back to the statement. Each statement node also has a pointer to the list of expressions that need to be evaluated before that statement can be executed. A boolean field is used to indicate that a breakpoint is set at the statement. Finally, an integer field is used by the editor to indicate how many lines are required to print the statement, including the space required by any nested statements.

For the almost forty different statement types in the AL language, the statement record makes use of approximately twenty-five variants. These different variants will now be described.

A special statement of type "program" is used to point to the statement making up the user's AL program. That statement is followed by an END statement which has a back pointer to the program statement.

Each BEGIN in the program is represented by a block statement. The block statement has a field for the string, if any, naming that block. This field points to an identifier record which in turn points to the string. There is a pointer to the block's parent block, that is, the next outermost surrounding block. There are two small integers used to hold the lexical level of the block, and the number of variables defined by the block. There is a pointer to the list of variables defined by the block. Finally, there is a pointer to the list of statements that make up the body of the block. The last statement in this list is the END statement which matches the BEGIN.

The END statement uses the same variant as the BEGIN statement. However, it uses only two of the fields: a pointer to the block identifier, if any, and a back pointer to the BEGIN statement it is paired with.

Declaration statements also use the block variant record. They use the pointer to the list of variables that they are declaring, and the integer telling how many variables make up the list. Note that, as mentioned earlier, each variable definition record is on two separate lists, making use of two different pointers in variable definition records.

For COBEGIN statements, a coblock variant is used. It has a pointer to the block identifier, a pointer to the list of statements to be executed in parallel, and an integer telling how many of these individual threads there are. A special node record of type colist is used to maintain the list of threads. Each colist node has a pointer to one of the threads, and pointers to the next and previous threads in the list, i.e. the colist nodes make up a doubly linked list. The statement list for each thread consists of the user's statement followed by a COEND statement. All of the threads in the coblock point to the same COEND statement.

COEND statements use the block variant and are identical to END statements. They use the pointer to the block identifier and have a back pointer to the corresponding COBEGIN statement.

FOR statements have pointers to four expressions specifying the variable to use, the initial and final values, and the step size. There is also a pointer to the statement making up the body of the FOR. This statement, in turn, points to an END statement which has a back pointer to the FOR statement.

The WHILE and UNTIL statements are similar to the FOR statement. They have one pointer to the conditional expression they test and another pointer to the statement composing the loop's body. This statement in turn points to an added END statement, complete with back pointer.

The IF statement has a pointer to the conditional expression it tests, and two pointers to statements: one for the THEN clause, and one for the ELSE clause. The ELSE pointer may be nil. Naturally both the THEN and ELSE statements point to an appended END statement with a back pointer to the parent IF statement.

The CASE statement is similar to the IF statement. There is a pointer to the selecting expression and another to the list of possible cases. Two integers tell how many of these cases there are and the allowable range of the case index expression. Numbered case statements are indicated by negating the range field. The case list is made up of special case list nodes. Each of these nodes has a pointer to the next node in the list and a pointer to the appropriate statement in the case list. For numbered case statements each case list node has an integer specifying the case label. ELSE is indicated by a value of -1. Bad labels, i.e. ones the parser could not parse as constants, as flagged with a value of -2. Each statement in the case list points to an END statement which has a back pointer to the parent CASE statement.

The PAUSE statement has one pointer to the expression specifying how long to pause.

The PRINT statement has one pointer to the list of expressions to be printed. This list is composed of list nodes, each pointing to an expression to be printed and to the next node in the list. This is the same as used by the QUERY operator described above. The PROMPT statement is exactly the same. The ABORT statement is also similar; however, ABORT uses an additional field. The debugger occasionally inserts ABORT statements into the program and needs to distinguish between them. The additional field specifies the debugging level associated with the ABORT statement. For all of the ABORT statements in the user's AL program this field is set to zero. The use of the specially inserted ABORT statements will be discussed in the section on the debugger.

Assignment statements have two pointers, one for the expression specifying the variable being assigned to, and one for the expression being assigned. This same variant is used for statements just consisting of a procedure call. In this case the pointer to the assignment variable is nil and the pointer to the expression being assigned points to the expression calling the procedure.

The RETURN statement has a pointer to the expression being returned. It also contains a pointer to the procedure definition node of the procedure whose body it is in.

The AFFIX statement has four pointers to expressions specifying the two variables being affixed, the explicit trans variable to hold the affixment relationship, and the transformation between the two variables. These last two pointers may be nil. There is also a boolean field used to indicate whether the affixment is rigid or not. The UNFIX statement uses the same variant, but only needs to specify the two pointers indicating the variables being unfixed.

The SIGNAL statement has a pointer to the expression specifying the event that is being signalled. The WAIT statement is treated similarly.

The same variant is used by all of the various motion statements: MOVE, OPERATE, OPEN, CLOSE, CENTER and STOP. It consists of a pointer to an expression specifying the control frame for the motion, and, for all but the STOP statement, a pointer to a list of clauses modifying the motion. Each clause is one of the following seventeen node records: departure, via, approach, destination, duration, speed factor, wobble, stop-wait time, nulling, zero wrist, clockwise, force frame, force, stiffness, gather, condition monitor, and comment.

Departure, approach, and destination nodes each have a pointer to the expression giving the appropriate location. Deproach points have an additional pointer to any statement specified with a THEN clause. This is the statement that would be executed during the motion when the arm passed through the deproach point. Actually, unless the statement specified was a SIGNAL statement, the following is the case: a new event condition monitor is created with the statement associated with the deproach point as its body. The deproach clause then points to this condition monitor.

Each via point has three pointers to expressions giving the location of the via point, and any associated velocity or duration specifications. There is also a pointer to any statement associated with the via. This is the same as described above for deproach points. Finally, there is a boolean field indicating whether the via point is one specified in a via list, e.g. "VIA a,b,c."

Duration clauses contain a pointer to an expression giving a duration time and to a field holding the duration relation, expressed as a subrange of the scalar type associated with the possible arithmetic operators. Possible duration relations are less than (upper bound specified), greater than (lower bound specified), and equal to (exact value specified). The duration specification for via points and for condition monitors also uses duration nodes.

Speed factor, wobble and stop-wait time nodes have a single pointer to an expression specifying their value. Nulling, zero wrist and clockwise nodes have a boolean field to indicate whether the condition they represent is to be done or not.

Force frame nodes have a pointer to the expression containing the force frame's location. They also have two boolean fields, one for whether the force frame is being specified in world or hand coordinates, and one to indicate that the force frame was automatically added during parsing, which is used by the editor so it does not display it.

Force nodes have two scalar fields. The first specifies what type of force is being specified, force, torque, or angular velocity, and also whether only the absolute magnitude is being specified. The second indicates the force relation: less than, equal to, or greater than. There are also three pointers to expressions to specify the force magnitude, the force direction vector, and the force frame being used.

The stiffness node has three expression pointers: the vector for the force spring constants, the vector for the torque spring constants, and the force frame specifying the center of compliance.

The gather node has a single integer field where the low order thirteen bits are used to specify which of the possible thirteen force/torque components are to be gathered.

For condition monitor nodes there is a pointer to the condition monitor statement record. There is an additional boolean field used to indicate whether the condition monitor is actually an error handler. Condition monitor statements will be described shortly.

Finally, the comment node uses the same leaf node variant as strings. It has a pointer to the comment string and an integer indicating the length of the comment.

Continuing with the variants of the statement record, the RETRY statement has two statement pointers: one to the motion statement to retry, and the other to the error handler enclosing the RETRY statement. There is also an integer giving the lexical level of the motion statement.

For condition monitor statements there is a pointer to the variable definition record of the variable associated with the condition monitor. Another pointer points to the statement to be executed when the condition monitor triggers. The conclusion statement in turn points to an added END statement that points back to the condition monitor statement. There are two boolean fields indicating whether the condition monitor is to be deferred and whether it is monitoring an expression. There is also a pointer to a node record specifying the condition to be monitored. This node may be an expression (includes event), duration, force, arrival, departing or error node type. The first three of these have already been discussed. An arrival node has a pointer to the variable definition record of the event that will be signalled upon the successful termination of the motion. No fields are needed by the departing node. The error node has a single pointer indicating the expression giving the error conditions that the error handler will attempt to handle. For error handlers the END appended to the conclusion statement points back to the associated motion statement rather than to the condition monitor itself.

The ENABLE and DISABLE statements both contain a pointer to the variable definition record of the label variable, which in turn points to a condition monitor statement.

The SETBASE statement has one pointer to an expression indicating which wrist is to be set. The WRIST statement has two pointers to expressions specifying the two vector variables to store the wrist readings in. It also has another expression pointer indicating which wrist is to be used.

COMMENT statements consist of a pointer to a string containing the comment and an integer to tell how many characters are in the comment string.

The DIMENSION statement has a pointer to the variable definition record of the variable being dimensioned, and a pointer to the dimensioning expression.

The DEFINE statement has a pointer to the variable definition record of the macro variable and another pointer to a list of variable definition records, one for each formal parameter used by the macro. A third pointer points to the list of tokens that make up the body of the macro. More will be said about these token records when parsing is discussed.

The REQUIRE statement contains a boolean field to indicate whether a source file or error modes are being specified. There is also a pointer to a string and an integer giving the string's length.

4.3 Interpreter

This section starts off discussing the various data types used by the interpreter. Then it moves on to look at the statement interpretation process, including a discussion of scheduling. Next, the mechanisms involved with affixment are detailed. Finally, the interaction between the interpreter and the arm servo module is discussed.

Interpreter Data Types

There are several types of records used by the interpreter when running a program. These include a descriptor record for each process, several records used to establish the dynamic environment information needed for the active variables, and the record type used for the messages passed between AL and the arm servos.

Process descriptor blocks. Whenever a new process is sprouted by entering a coblock statement, by creating a new condition monitor, or by calling a procedure, a new process descriptor block (or pdb) record is created and associated with the process. This process descriptor record is used to specify the process's state, its stack, where it is in the program, and various other information. Because a process may be swapped out at any time, all of the information relating to it must be contained in its process descriptor.

The process's state is contained in several pdb fields. One field contains the current status of the process. Possible status values are: not active, now running, waiting to run, waiting for terminal input, waiting for an event to be signalled, waiting for a motion to finish, waiting for a force condition to occur, waiting for a called procedure to return, waiting for all of the threads of a coblock to finish, and sleeping for some duration.

Another pdb field contains the priority at which the process is being run. The priority consists of two parts, the debugger recursion level and the priority within that level. These are stored as the sum of the debugging level times ten plus the base-level priority.

The main program is run at priority zero. Condition monitors are run at a priority one greater than that of the process that defines them. If the main program is interrupted and a new one sprouted by the debugger, then the new process would be run at a priority of ten, i.e. at a debugging level of one, with a base priority of zero. Only those processes at the current debugging level are scheduled for execution.

Each process has a stack, composed of leaf nodes, the top node of which is pointed to by a field in the pdb. This stack is primarily used for holding intermediate values during expression evaluation.

Two other pdb fields point to the statement currently being interpreted and to the expression node, if any, currently being evaluated. Another integer field contains mode information specifying which step the process had reached in interpreting the current statement. More will be said about all of these fields when the basic interpreter loop is discussed below.

To provide access to the values of active variables, each pdb has a pointer to an environment header. Those records used to describe environments are described below. There is also a field specifying the lexical level of the current environment.

There are two pointers that point to other process descriptor blocks. One is used to connect pdbs in the same queue into a list. The other is used to keep a single list of all processes that currently exist. This is used by the debugger to display the active processes when the user asks for a trace. It is also used to allow old processes to be flushed when popping up a debugging level or when restarting. Another field used by the debugger contains the line number in the program of the statement that the process is currently executing.

There is another pointer used to remember the device currently being controlled by the process.

For condition monitors there is a pointer to the condition monitor's control block, which specifies the condition monitor's current state and also points back to its defining statement.

A boolean field is used to tell whether the process is a procedure or not. Two variants exist based on it. For procedures there is a pointer to the pdb of the process that called the procedure, used when returning, and a pointer to the procedure's definition node. The other variant has a pointer to the event to signal when the process terminates, used for the threads in a coblock, and a pointer to the statement where the process was defined, used by the debugger to reclaim immediate statements. Condition monitors also make use of the pdb pointer field in the procedure variant, using it to point to their parent process.

Environment-related records. When a new block is entered, any variables declared in it must be created. The way this is done by the AL interpreter is to create a new environment (or display) which will contain the values of the block's variables. Each variable has its own environment entry. These entries are grouped together by a list of environment records, which in turn are accessed through an environment header record.

The basic environment record consists of an array pointing to ten variable environment entry records and a pointer to the next environment record in the list.

Each process has a pointer in its pdb to the environment header record of the current environment. This header record has a pointer to the next outermost environment. The outermost environment consists of the predeclared system variables. Another field in the header tells the number of variables in use. An array points to the first five environment records, providing direct access to them. A boolean field indicates whether the environment is associated with a block or with a procedure. Two variants provide a pointer of the appropriate type to either the block statement or the procedure definition node. They are used to access the lexical level of the environment.

Each variable definition contains the lexical level at which it is defined, and an offset into the block's list of variables. To look up a variable the first step is to move up to the header of the environment at the proper lexical level. Then the offset is divided by ten. The integer quotient indicates which of the environment records contains the pointer to the proper environment entry for the variable. If this quotient is less than five the environment can be directly accessed from the header record. Otherwise, the appropriate number of environment records in the environment list are run through, starting with the fifth one. Once the environment record is located, the offset modulo ten is used to access the variable's environment entry record, and, hence, the variable's value.

The environment entry record consists of a field holding the variable's type and appropriate fields to hold/access its value. For the basic data types it is quite similar to the leaf node: scalars are stored directly, vectors and transes have a pointer to the vector or trans, and strings have a field to hold the number of characters in the string and also a pointer to the start of the string. Events point to an event record which keeps track of which processes are waiting on the event. For frames there is a pointer to the frame record associated with the variable. For condition monitors there is a pointer to the condition monitor's control block record. A detailed description of event, frame and condition monitor control block records appears below.

Procedure variables have two pointers. One is to the procedure's definition node, while the other points to the environment in which the procedure is defined.

For parameters passed to a procedure by reference, the environment entry of the formal variable in the procedure points back to the environment entry of the variable which was passed as the actual parameter in the procedure call.

For array variables the environment entry record has two pointers. The first is to an environment header; this points in turn through environment records to the environment entries, one per element of the array. These elements are stored in row major order. The second pointer of the array's environment record points to a list of array bounds. This is similar to the list of array bound definition nodes that the array's variable definition record points to, except that now the bound's actual value is stored. Each array bound value node contains three integers and a pointer to the next node in the bounds list. The integers give the upper and lower bounds of this subscript, along with the constant to multiply this subscript's offset by when computing the linear offset into the array's list of environment entries. More formally, for an n-dimensional array A the linear offset for $A[I_1, I_2, \ldots, I_n]$ is

$$C_1(I_1 - L_1) + C_2(I_2 - L_2) + \ldots + C_n(I_n - L_n)$$

and

$$C_1 = (U_2 - L_2)C_2$$
$$C_2 = (U_3 - L_3)C_3$$
$$\ldots$$
$$C_n = 1$$

where I_j is the jth subscript index, C_j is the constant associated with that index, U_j and L_j are the upper and lower bounds for that index.

Event records. Associated with each event variable is an event record. This record has an integer field indicating the number of times the event has been signaled. Negative values indicate that many processes are waiting on the event. These waiting processes are pointed to by the second field of the event record. It points to the pdb of the process to wake up the next time it is signaled. This pdb in turn points to the next process waiting on the event.

The final field in the event record is used to link all the current events onto one big list. There are no pointers in the pdb telling which event the process is waiting on, so searching the list of all events is the only way to remove a process from an event's wait queue.

Frame records. Each frame variable and device has a frame record associated with it to either hold the variable's value or to specify how that value can be calculated. Each frame record has a back pointer to the variable's definition record. Each frame also has a pointer to any calculator nodes, which are used to affix two frames together. Calculator nodes are described below in the discussion of affixment.

There are two major variants of the frame record: one for devices, and one for regular frame variables. Devices have an integer field containing the mechanism number that the arm code associates with the device. There are currently two sub-variants for devices: one for scalar devices (simple hands), and one for frames (arms). These variants hold values associated with the last motion commanded for the device. For both, the destination position is remembered, as a scalar in one case, and as a pointer to a trans in the other. Frame devices also have two other trans pointers to hold the two deproach points associated with the motion: the departure and approach points.

For regular frame variables there is a pointer to the frame's value, along with an integer flag set to zero if the value is currently valid. If the flag is non-zero then the frame value must be calculated by using the affixment information pointed to by the frame record. During this process the flag is used as a time stamp to avoid loops while tracking through the affixment graph. Frames that are affixed to devices are specially marked with a pointer to the device's frame record, and an integer count of the length of the affixment chain connecting the frame and the device. There is also a pointer to a trans representing any deproach point that has been associated with the frame. Currently, this is a relic, which can be set, but is never used.

Condition monitor control blocks. Each condition monitor has a control block record associated with it. This record has two boolean fields, one specifying whether the condition monitor is currently enabled and the other specifying whether it is now running, i.e. the condition it has been monitoring has triggered. There is a pointer to the pdb of the process associated with the condition monitor. Another pointer points to the statement defining the monitor.

For force-sensing condition monitors there is a pointer to the event that will be used by the arm servo code to signal that the desired force condition has occurred. An integer field holds the bits used to indicate to the arm code along which axis the force or torque is to be monitored, along with whether to use the absolute magnitude of the force, and if the triggering is on the force exceeding or going below the specified threshold.

There is also a pointer to any old control block that may have been preempted. Using the execute command the debugger may attempt to execute a statement that will enable a condition monitor that had been previously enabled at a lower debugging level. If this happens the interpreter will create a new instantiation of the condition monitor, complete with new control block. The condition monitor's environment entry will then be made to point to the new control block, which in turn will point to the old one.

Message records. The AL interpreter communicates with the arm servo module via messages. The current message record has been specially tailored to the small size messages that RSX will pass between tasks. Each message has a field specifying the command type of the message being passed. A boolean field is used to convey success or failure of an operation. There are two record variants. The first has two integers specifying the mechanism number of the device being referred to and any bits that may be needed. A third field contains a pointer to an event to use to signal AL when the command has concluded or some condition has occurred. There are four reals used to pass over other information, which differs from command to command. Several sub-variants are used to give these real fields different names. The other variant consists of six reals: either two vectors, or half of a trans. More will be said about the interaction between the interpreter and the arm code at the end of this section.

Interpreter Operation

In the design of the AL interpreter a major consideration was that the AL language provides for concurrent execution of statements through constructs like COBEGIN blocks, condition monitors and code associated with intermediate points in a motion. A process can block by initiating a motion, requesting input from the terminal, waiting for an event to be signalled, going to sleep, etc. When a process blocks, the interpreter must swap it out and swap in some other process. Things are further complicated by the fact that any expression can contain a call on a procedure, which might contain a statement that will cause the process to block.

Since AL is implemented in standard Pascal, which does not support concurrency, the interpreter itself must explicitly handle this scheduling of the various processes. In doing this, the information needed to specify the current context of a process cannot be stored on the Pascal runtime system's call or value stacks. Instead, it must all be stored explicitly in data structures associated with the process, hence the use of process descriptor blocks.

The effect of all this is that the interpreter itself is written in a fundamentally iterative manner, rather than recursively. Each time through, the main interpreter loop performs just one "atomic" operation. These "atomic" operations range from a single algebraic operator in an expression, to partial or full statement execution. Any routines that the main loop calls must return control to it before the next operation is performed.

Each process has three fields in its pdb which specify what the process is currently doing. These are a pointer to the current statement, an integer specifying which step the interpreter has reached in executing that statement, and a pointer to the next expression to evaluate.

Interpretation proceeds in the following manner. If the expression pointer is not nil then the interpreter will dispatch to a routine to evaluate the current operation in the expression and advance the pointer to the next one. If the expression pointer is nil then the interpreter looks at the type of the current statement and passes control to the appropriate routine. This routine performs the required actions and either changes the state (or mode) field in the pdb, or advances to the next statement.

Expression Evaluation

As mentioned earlier, each statement has a pointer to a list of all the expressions that need to be evaluated before the statement can be executed. Each process has its own value stack which is used to hold the values of these expressions, along with any intermediate values that are calculated while evaluating the expressions. The first step in interpreting a statement is to set the expression pointer in the pdb to the head of the expression list for the statement. After all of the expressions have been calculated, the statement can be interpreted. The computed values are then popped from the value stack when they are needed.

The procedure for evaluating a node in the expression list is as follows. If the expression pointer is to a constant leaf node then a copy of the leaf node is created and pushed on the stack. If it is a variable leaf node then the variable's environment entry is looked up using the level and offset values in the associated variable definition record. If it is an array variable the proper array element is accessed using the subscript indices on the top of the value stack. A new leaf node is created to hold the variable's value and pushed on the value stack. For frame variables the current value may need to be first computed using the affixment information.

If the expression pointer is to an expression node then the first step is to get the operator's current arguments. These are popped from the value stack or, if the argument was a constant, obtained directly from the expression tree. After obtaining the arguments, the specified operation is performed upon them and the result pushed onto the value stack for future use by another operator or in interpreting the associated statement.

For procedure calls, more needs to be done. First, the procedure variable is looked up. Then a new process descriptor block for the procedure is created. It contains a pointer to the current process's pdb, so control can be returned to it later. A new environment is then created to hold the parameters for the procedure. These are then bound with the procedure's actual parameters. For reference parameters, the new environment entry record will contain a pointer to the environment entry of the variable being passed to the procedure. If the quantity being passed by reference is not a variable then it is changed to being passed by value. The parent of the procedure's environment is set to the environment of the block that contains the procedure's definition, a pointer to which is contained in the environment entry for the procedure. The new pdb for the procedure is set up to commence execution with the first statement in the procedure's body, and then made the active process.

There are several other operators that need special mention. QUERY first prints out those expressions specified in its print list, popping their values from the value stack if needed, followed by a prompt message asking the user to "type Y or N." It then puts the process into the read queue to await input from the terminal. After the user types in a line the interpreter will awaken the process, which will see that input is awaiting it, and push the appropriate boolean value onto the value stack. If the user types something other than "Y" or "N" the prompt message will be repeated, and the process will again wait for terminal input. Similarly INSCALAR asks for a real number and goes to sleep until the user enters a number.

The two operators, DAC and ADC, require interaction with the arm code module. One of the hardware devices connected to AL is a hardware interface to sixty-four A/D and four D/A channels. Access to these channels is through the arm code module. For DAC the user specifies the channel and the required output voltage. This information is sent in a message to the arm code for it to perform. Likewise, for ADC the channel number is sent over in a request to read the current value, and the value sent back in the arm code's reply is pushed onto the value stack.

Statement Interpretation

Once all of the expressions associated with a statement have been evaluated and their values stored on the stack, the statement proper can be dealt with. For most types of statements this is a one step process. For example, for an assignment statement, first the environment entry for the variable being assigned to is looked up, the value being assigned is popped off the stack, the environment entry updated with the new value, and finally the statement pointer advanced to the next statement and the mode field set to zero.

For other statement types this can involve several steps. For example, in interpreting a PROMPT statement the first step is to print out any expressions in its print list. Then a prompt message asking the user to "type P to proceed" is printed and the process put into the read queue to wait for the user to enter input to the terminal. The next step occurs after a line has been typed and the interpreter awakens the process. If the character is a "P" then the statement pointer is advanced to the next statement and the mode field reset to zero; otherwise, the prompt message is repeated and the process again goes to sleep while awaiting input.

Each of the various AL statements will now be discussed in turn. For those that are straightforward not much will be said, though some deserve special mention. Unless otherwise stated, for all of these statements the last step in interpreting them is to advance the statement pointer in the process descriptor block to the next statement.

Surrounding each program is a statement of special type, program. Interpretation of it resets the interpreter to its initial state, breaking any old affixments between system variables and resetting system variables such as speed _ factor to their original values. The pdb statement pointer is then set to the body of the program.

When a new block is entered, a new environment record is allocated to hold the values of the block's variables, if any. This involves creating a new environment header, with its parent pointer set to the old environment, and updating the pdb to point to this new header record. An environment entry is created for each variable defined by the block. For each condition monitor a new pdb is created to be used later when the condition monitor is enabled. The statement pointer is then set to the first statement in the block.

A variety of different actions occur when an END statement is encountered. For those ENDs corresponding to an explicit END statement in the user's program, the variables defined by the block are flushed, and the process waits for any condition monitors that are still running to finish. As mentioned earlier in the discussion of the internal program representation, END statements are also created to terminate all statement lists. These implicitly defined END statements contain a back pointer to the parent of the list of statements, and the action that is performed is determined by the parent statement's type. If the parent statement is the surrounding program statement, then the interpreter is done running the program, and control is returned to the editor/debugger. For some statements, such as IF and CASE, the pdb statement pointer is advanced to the statement following the parent statement. For others, such as the various loop statements—FOR, WHILE, and DO UNTIL—control passes back to the parent statement with the mode field of the pdb set appropriately. Finally, for condition monitors, they are either rescheduled or put to sleep, depending on whether they are still enabled or not. More will be said about each of these situations when the parent statement type is discussed below.

For COBEGIN/COEND blocks, the first step is to create pdbs for each thread, and then to schedule them for execution. The parent process also creates an event to be signalled by each of the threads when they finish, and then goes to sleep waiting for this event to be signalled the appropriate number of times. As each thread finishes, the last statement it encounters is a COEND which terminates the process and updates the count of the number of remaining threads. If this was the last active thread, then the parent process is awakened and it will continue execution with the next statement.

For an IF statement, the IF condition is popped from the stack and if it is true (non-zero) then the pdb statement pointer is set to the THEN clause; otherwise it is set to the ELSE clause. If the IF has no ELSE clause then control proceeds to the next statement after the IF. An END statement follows both the THEN and ELSE clause statements: when it is executed control is passed to the statement following the parent IF statement.

The CASE statement is handled similarly. First the CASE index is popped off the stack and the CASE list searched for that index value. If one is found, then control passes to it. If no matching index was found, and it is a numbered CASE statement, then an ELSE labeled statement is searched for, and, if found, run. Otherwise, an error message saying that the case index is not valid is printed, and control is passed to the statement following the CASE. Again, each statement in the case list is followed by an END statement which, when executed, passes control to the statement following the parent CASE statement.

When a WHILE statement is encountered, the interpreter pops the WHILE condition's value from the stack and, if it is true, sets the pdb statement pointer to the body of the WHILE. This body is followed by an added END statement which resets the pdb statement pointer back to the parent WHILE statement, so the condition will again be evaluated, and the loop continued for as long as necessary. When the condition becomes false, control passes to the statement after the WHILE.

The UNTIL statement is similar. First, though, the body of the loop is executed. When it finishes, an END statement is encountered that passes control back to the UNTIL statement, with the mode field set so the interpreter will now evaluate the UNTIL condition. If the UNTIL condition's value is false, the loop statement is again executed; otherwise, control passes to the following statement.

The first step in interpreting a FOR statement is to assign the initial value to the FOR variable and to store away the step and final values on the stack. A FOR value node is used to hold both the step size and a pointer to the environment entry of the FOR variable. Next, the interpreter tests if the initial value is less than the final value (or greater than it if the step size is negative), and, if so, executes the body of the FOR loop. The body terminates when it encounters an END statement that will increment the FOR variable and return control to the FOR statement with the mode field set so the interpreter will again test to see if the loop has finished or not. When it finishes, the pdb statement pointer is advanced to the statement after the FOR.

The PAUSE statement pops the time to pause off the stack, and puts the process to sleep for that amount of time. The sleep queue is described below.

The PRINT statement types its print list on the user's screen, popping any needed values from the stack. The ABORT statement similarly deals with its print list, but, before doing so, it signals the arm code to halt any motions currently in progress. The ABORT statement finally stops the interpreter and returns control to the editor/debugger. If the user then tells the debugger to proceed, execution will continue with the statement following the ABORT statement.

The AFFIX and UNFIX statements are described in more detail below in the discussion of affixment. AFFIX causes an affixment to be made between the two named frames with the specified relationship. UNFIX breaks this affixment.

When a RETURN statement is encountered, any value being returned is popped from the stack and the rest of the stack flushed. All of the variables defined in blocks in the procedure body are destroyed, along with the procedure's parameters. The procedure's pdb is then also flushed and the calling process's pdb once again made active. The returned value is then pushed onto the calling process's stack. If the RETURN was not in the body of a procedure, it is ignored and a warning message printed. A special case of the RETURN statement occurs when the user, through the debugger, issues a RETURN statement for immediate execution. In this case, if the interrupted process was in a procedure body, a return from it to its caller is performed. Later, when the process continues, it will be from after the call to the procedure.

For SIGNAL the indicated event's environment entry is looked up, and the wait-count field incremented by one. If there are any processes currently waiting on the event, then the first of these is awakened and made active. If its priority is greater than the signalling process's then the signalling process is swapped out; otherwise the newly awakened process is placed in the run queue.

WAIT also looks up the event's environment entry and the wait-count field is decremented by one. If it is still positive, then the event has already been signalled and there is no need to wait. If it is negative then the process is added to the event's wait list. The wait list is ordered by decreasing process priority, with processes at the same priority stored in a first-in, first-out fashion.

SIGNAL and WAIT have a different effect if a global flag has been set by the debugger specifying that the user has requested "nowait" mode. If that is the case, then, rather than actually signalling an event, the SIGNAL statement will print out a message saying that it "WOULD SIGNAL EVENT: foo," where foo is the name of the event being signalled. In nowait mode the WAIT statement would print out that it "WOULD WAIT FOR EVENT: foo," then it would act just like the PROMPT statement described above, printing out the message: "TYPE P TO PROCEED:" and waiting for the user to type a "P."

Condition monitor statements can be encountered in three different states. The first is when the interpreter statement pointer advances to a statement condition monitor. The condition monitor is then enabled, which is done by placing the process associated with the condition monitor in the run queue. The interpreter will then schedule this process. The second state for condition monitors is when they have been enabled and need to be set up to test for their triggering condition. Duration condition monitors are placed in the sleep queue. Those that wait for events are placed on the appropriate event's wait list. Force-sensing monitors send over a message to the arm code specifying the triggering force condition and the event to signal if and when the condition occurs, then the monitor is placed on the event's wait list. For expression condition monitors, the expression's value is popped from the stack and tested. If it is not yet true, the condition monitor is put to sleep for a short while (currently 100 milliseconds), at which time it will be evaluated again. If it is true, then the monitor triggers. The final state for condition monitors is after they have triggered. The interpreter checks that the condition monitor is still enabled and if so, control passes to the monitor's conclusion. Otherwise the monitor is placed in the null queue. The conclusion of the condition monitor finishes by encountering an END statement, pointing back to the monitor statement. If the condition monitor has been re-enabled, then the pdb will be set so the condition monitor again sets up its triggering condition. Otherwise, the process is suspended and placed in the null queue.

The ENABLE statement looks up the condition monitor associated with the given label, and, if one is found, it is then enabled. The DISABLE statement is the same, except that if the condition monitor is found, it is disabled.

When interpreting a motion statement, be it a MOVE, OPERATE, OPEN, CLOSE, or CENTER, a number of steps must be taken. The first of these is to determine which device is being specified and to store it in the process's pdb. Then, any force specifications used during the motion must be sent over to the arm servo module, and any associated condition monitors enabled. The process may then be swapped out in order to set up the condition monitors. When it is continued, the second step is to send over the other specifications of the requested trajectory: the destination and intermediate points, duration and speed factor terms, etc. Also sent over is an event to use to signal when the motion has finished. The motion is then commenced, and the process put on the event's wait list. After the arm code signals that the motion has terminated, the third step is to disable any still active condition monitors, which may require sleeping until they finish running, and check whether the motion was successful or whether there was an error. If there has been an error, then a check is made to see whether an error handler had been specified for the error that has occurred. If so, it is run; otherwise an appropriate error message is printed and the user asked whether to continue, try again, or break to the debugger. The process is put into the read queue awaiting the user's response. After getting a reply, the fourth, and final, state takes the appropriate action.

In an error handler, if the interpreter encounters a RETRY statement it will flush any environments out to the body of the error handler and set the pdb statement pointer back to the parent motion statement. A RETRY statement anywhere else is just ignored.

For SETBASE and WRIST, an appropriate message is sent to the arm code, and, for WRIST, a reply is awaited containing the current force wrist readings.

Other statements, such as declarations, macro definitions, comments, requires, etc., have no effect during interpretation and are ignored.

Process Queues

The interpreter has several different queues which are used to keep track of the individual processes that may be running at any point in the user's AL program. The first queue to discuss is the active processes queue, or run queue. All currently running processes are members of this queue. The process that is currently running has a pointer to its pdb, while another pointer is used for the list of processes waiting to run. The list is ordered by priority—higher priority processes coming first—and within each priority level by when the process was added to the queue—

those entered earliest are ahead of later entries. This same ordering is also used in the other process queues.

Those processes sleeping for some duration of time are placed on the clock queue. This queue consists of a list of wait list nodes, each of which has a pointer to the next node in the list, another pointer to the list of processes to awaken, and the number of clock ticks to wait before awakening them. The wait time stored in each node is the time to wait after the preceding node in the list. At any point while interpreting the program, the system is only concerned with the time until the first node in the clock queue needs to be awakened.

A limited queue exists for those processes awaiting input from the user. Before a process requests input, it checks if any other processes at its debugging level are already awaiting a user response. If so, they go to sleep for a short time and then try again when they wake up. When no other process at the same level is using the terminal, the process is put into the read queue. When a line of input has been entered, the first process in the queue is awakened. Put another way, only one process can grab the terminal for input at a time. However, if it is interrupted by the user, for example by typing a ↑C to return control to the debugger, then any new processes the user starts with a higher debugging level will be able to use the terminal. When the interrupted process is resumed, the interpreter will repeat the appropriate prompt message to remind the user that the program is awaiting input.

As already discussed, each event has its own wait queue for those processes that are waiting for the event to be signalled.

Finally, those processes that are currently inactive, such as a disabled condition monitor, are in the null queue, which is not explicitly kept.

Process Scheduling

Finally, the complete inner loop of the interpreter can be described. The first thing the interpreter does is to check whether any messages from the arm servo module have been received, and, if so, they are processed. Possible messages are errors, which the interpreter prints out, and signals that either a motion is done, an intermediate point reached, or a force triggered, all of which result in the process waiting for that event being awakened and placed in the run queue. When a process is added to the active list, a check is made whether its priority is greater than that of the currently active process, and, if so, a flag is set indicating that the interpreter needs to swap out the current process and reschedule a process from the run queue. In the case of a motion being done, in addition to waking up the process, a node is placed on its stack indicating if an error occurred to terminate the motion prematurely.

Next, the interpreter checks whether it is time for the first entry in the clock queue to be awakened. If so, all of the processes associated with it are added to the run queue, and the node removed from the clock queue. If there is another entry in the clock queue, then the time until it should be awakened is noted, and a request placed with the operating system to signal the interpreter when that length of time has elapsed.

It should be noted that various interrupt routines set appropriate flags when a message is received or a specified time interval has elapsed. The main interpreter loop then only needs to check those flags to see whether it needs to process the message, or deal with the clock queue.

Another flag is set whenever a process is added to the run queue that has a priority higher than that of the currently running process. This flag is also set if, during statement interpretation, the currently executing process blocks and is swapped out. When the interpreter sees this flag set, the current process is swapped out and the highest priority process in the run queue is scheduled to be run.

Next, the interpreter checks whether any process at the current debugging level is in the read queue waiting for input. If so, it then checks whether any characters have been typed and places them in its line buffer. If the character typed was a backspace or rubout, then the last character placed in the buffer is deleted. If a carriage return has been typed, then the process waiting for the input is awakened and scheduled to be run immediately.

Then the interpreter is ready to actually perform the next step in the interpretation of the program. If the pdb's expression pointer is not nil then that expression node is evaluated, and the expression pointer advanced. Otherwise if the mode field is zero, indicating the interpreter is starting a new statement, then the expression pointer is set to the head of the list of expressions that need to be evaluated for that statement, and the mode field is then advanced to one. This is true for all statement types except DO-UNTIL and condition monitors, which are handled slightly differently. If both the expression pointer is nil and the mode field is non-zero, then the routine associated with the current statement's type is called.

Finally, the interpreter checks whether the last step advanced the program to a new statement that has a breakpoint associated with it, or whether a ↑C has been typed. If either of these conditions is the case, then the interpreter returns control to the editor/debugger. Otherwise, the interpreter continues in its loop, interpreting the rest of the program.

Affixment

Affixment in AL provides a mechanism to declare a spatial relationship between two frames. When either of them is assigned a new value, the system will automatically update the position of the other to maintain the declared relationship. Of course, a frame may be affixed to many other frames and the resulting affixment structure is a graph, which may contain cycles.

The current affixment structure is stored in calculator nodes associated with the affixed frames. Each frame has a pointer to a list of these calculator nodes, each of which describes an affixment between that frame and another. The calculator node has two boolean fields indicating whether the affixment is rigid or nonrigid, and whether this frame is the parent frame in the affixment or not. There is also a pointer to the other frame. A third boolean field distinguishes two variant records. It indicates whether the transform relating the two frames is stored in an explicitly named trans variable. Two variants exist to point to the trans, either directly or indirectly through the trans variable's environment entry. Each affixment requires two calculator nodes, one for the calculator list of each of the two frames.

When one frame is assigned a new value, rather than immediately update all of those frames affixed to it (and all the frames affixed to those frames), the other frames are marked as being invalid. This is done by using the validity field in the frame record. This field is zero if the frame has a pointer to a currently valid value. Non-zero values indicate the frame is not currently pointing to a valid value; moreover, the actual non-zero value is used as a time stamp to indicate whether the frame has been visited during any traversal of the affixment graph. In the case of an assignment to a frame that is not affixed to any other frames—i.e. its calculator list is not empty—the first step is to increment the current "time." Then the frame being assigned to is marked invalid, as are all the frames on its calculator list. The marking process is recursive; after a frame is marked as being invalid, so are all of the frames on its calculator list. By checking to see whether the validity field is equal to the current time, frames which have already been marked are detected. Finally, the original frame has its value pointer set to the new value, and it is marked as now being valid.

The arms, and any frames affixed to them, are marked as being permanently invalid. This is to assure that the arm's current position will always be used when referencing these dynamic frames. The user's program cannot explicitly assign a value to a dynamic frame; only values based on the hardware sensors as read by the arm servo module are used.

When an attempt is made to get the value of a frame that is currently marked as valid, the pointer to its current value is immediately returned. If the frame is not currently valid, then its value must be computed from the affixment structure. As a first step, a quick check is made to see whether any of the frames directly affixed to it are currently valid. This is done by running down its calculator list and checking whether the other frame associated with each calculator node is currently valid. If so, then its value is multiplied by the transform relating the two frames to obtain the desired value. Actually, depending on the parent field in the calculator node, either the trans or its inverse is used. If none of the frames directly affixed to it is currently valid, then an attempt will be made to validate each of them, in turn, until a valid value is found. Then the known transformations connecting the valid frame with the desired one are used to obtain its current value. During this process, the interpreter again makes use of time stamps to indicate that an attempt has been made to validate a given frame, so it need not repeat itself. While searching for a valid frame, if a frame associated with a device is encountered, then a message will be sent to the arm code module requesting its current value.

The above method of invalidating and validating frames is slightly complicated by the asymmetry of nonrigid affixments. An example of this type of affixment is a plate on a tray. When the tray moves, so does the plate, but moving the plate does not affect the tray. If a frame is invalidated on the tray's side of the affixment structure then the plate's frame would also be invalidated. However, if a frame on the plate's side of the affixment is invalidated, then no frame on the tray's side is affected; instead, the transform between the plate and the tray is updated to reflect the new relationship. When trying to get a value for the plate, the value of the tray may be used. However, the plate's value is not used when attempting to validate the tray's frame.

The process to affix two frames is as follows. If the transform relating the two frames is not explicitly given, then it is calculated using the current values of the two frames. Then if the frames are already affixed to each other, the old calculator nodes are located and modified with the new affixment relation; otherwise, new calculator nodes are created and added to the frames' calculator lists.

To unfix two frames, the calculator nodes connecting them are spliced out of the two frames' calculator lists, and then flushed. Before doing this, however, an attempt is made to get valid values for both frames. If this validation were not done, it is likely that no value could be calculated for one of the frames, since all of the frames on that side of the broken affixment might be currently marked as invalid.

The above process of making and breaking affixments is complicated by the introduction of dynamic frames, i.e. devices and those frames affixed to devices. When a frame is affixed either directly to an arm, or indirectly through a frame affixed to an arm, it also becomes dynamic. All the frames previously affixed to it are also marked as now being dynamic. For nonrigid affixments, such as the plate on a tray example used above, if the plate side has become dynamic, then the affixment between the plate and tray is broken. If instead the tray had been the frame that was affixed, then the affixment with the plate would remain unchanged, and the plate's side of the affixment would also be marked as now being dynamic. The interpreter keeps track of which arm a dynamic frame is affixed to, and how long the affixment chain is between the frame and the arm. Two arms cannot currently be affixed together either directly or indirectly through other connected frames.

The effect of dynamic frames, when breaking an affixment with an UNFIX statement, is to cause the frame further from the device, and all the frames it is still affixed to, to be marked as being no longer dynamic. While that is being done, a check is made to be sure that they are not affixed to the device through some other affixment path. If so, they are re-marked as being dynamic.

Interpreter–Arm Interaction

The interpreter interfaces to the arm servo process via message passing. Any time the interpreter needs the current position of a device it must send a message to the arm servo requesting that information. It then waits for the servo process to reply. For an actual motion, a series of messages is usually required. First, the interpreter will specify whether there is any force-sensing to be done, then send over any stiffness or bias force specifications, and then send a description of the desired motion consisting of destination, intermediate points, velocities and segment durations, overall speed, etc. Once all the motion specifications have been sent, the arm process will commence the motion and the interpreter process initiating the motion will block until the arm process sends a message to signal that the motion has terminated. During the course of the motion, the arm process may also send messages to signal that a force threshold has been exceeded or that an intermediate point has been reached. These will cause the interpreter to wake up whatever process had been waiting on that event.

There are approximately thirty different message types currently passed between the interpreter and the arm module. These include commands to initialize and calibrate the arms, kill the arm servo process, get a device's current value, abort all motions, stop an individual device's motion, initiate a motion, pass a description of a point in a motion, start a center or operate operation, signal a motion is done, signal some point or force condition has been reached, read the value of a device's joints, directly command a joint motion, set up force sensing for a motion, indicate a particular force to test for, stop testing for a force, introduce a bias force, turn off a bias force, set the stiffnesses to be used by an arm, zero or read the force wrist, gather data on forces encountered, ship over the gathered data, read an a/d, write to a d/a, cause an arm to float, and, finally, report errors.

When sending some of the above messages, several smaller message packets may need to be sent to convey the desired information. For example, it takes two packets to send over each trans. A typical intermediate point in a motion would require three packets: one to indicate what sort of point is being specified and two to pass over the trans giving the point's location.

Generally, all interpreter-arm interactions are initiated by the interpreter. The only exceptions to this are errors that come up while preparing to start a motion and events sent back to signal that either a motion has finished, a force condition has triggered, or an intermediate point in a motion has been reached. All other messages that the interpreter receives are the immediate result of a request it sent to the arm module.

4.4   Editor

This section begins with a description of the record types used by the editor in parsing and editing the user's AL program. Then the routines to support editor operations, such as displaying the program, repositioning the cursor, and modifying the parse tree, are discussed. Included in the discussion of modifying the parse tree is a description of the various parsing methods used by the editor.

Editor Data Types

There are three types of records relating to parsing that are used by the editor. These are records for reserved words, identifiers, and tokens. Associated with each reserved word in the AL language is a reserved word record. Each reserved word record consists of a pointer to a string holding the characters in the reserved word, an integer field specifying how many characters long the string is, and two other fields describing what type of reserved word it is. The first of these fields classifies the reserved word as either a statement keyword (e.g. IF, FOR, MOVE), a filler keyword (e.g. ABOUT, BY, ELSE, WITH), a clause related keyword (e.g. APPROACH, DURATION, WOBBLE), a data type (e.g. SCALAR, EVENT, ARRAY), and arithmetic operator (e.g. "+," MAX, SIN, SQRT), or as an editor command (e.g. GET, SAVE, PROCEED). A variant record type exists for each of these classes of keywords. Each has a single field of the appropriate scalar type to specify an internal token used to represent the reserved word. Each reserved word record has one final field which is used to link together reserved words. The various reserved words are hashed, based on which letter of the alphabet they start with, onto twenty-seven lists.

An identifier record is associated with each user variable and with each predeclared system variable and constant. (These were mentioned briefly in the section on internal representation.) Each identifier record points to a string containing the variable's name and has an integer field specifying the string's length. For predefined system variables and constants, another field points to the appropriate variable definition record; this field is nil for user variables. A final field is used to link together identifiers. Like reserved words, identifiers are hashed on their initial letter onto twenty-six lists.

During parsing, lexical tokens are passed about in token records. Each token record consists of a pointer or scalar type specifying the token. One field indicates the token's type: reserved word, identifier, constant, delimiter, comment, label, or macro parameter. Each of these types has its own variant record type. For reserved words, one field specifies the reserved word type: statement, filler, clause, declaration, operator or editor command. Another field indicates which reserved word, of the appropriate type, has been encountered. For identifiers, there is a pointer to the appropriate identifier record. Likewise, for constants there is a pointer to a leaf node containing the scalar constant's value. For delimiters, the token record contains the delimiting character. Each comment token type contains a pointer to a string holding the comment, and an integer field indicating its length. For labels and macro parameters there is a pointer to the associated variable definition record. Macro parameter variables occur only in the body of a macro. Each token record has one additional field which is used for macros to point to the next token in the macro body. More will be said about macros below.

There are two other record types used by the editor. The first of these is used by the display routines to specify the characters in each displayed line of the program. Each line record has three fields. The first is a pointer to other line records. The other two are integers indicating where in the display array the line starts, and how long it is. The display array is described below.

The final editor-related record type is the cursor record used to specify a point in the parse tree. Each cursor record has two integer fields specifying the line number associated with this point in the program, and the indentation depth at that point. A boolean field indicates whether the cursor is pointing to a statement or not and is used to select between two variants. Each variant contains a pointer either to the appropriate statement or node record. An array of these cursor records is used to describe the current cursor position.

Editor Operation

The editor operates on the parse tree representation of the user's AL program. The basic editor command loop consists of the user entering a command, which is echoed in the echo window, and the editor then executing the command, making any required changes in the program's parse tree and also adjusting the display window into the program if necessary. In the course of executing a command, the editor may need to invoke various parsing routines to read in an AL statement, clause, or expression.

The various editor routines can be classified as those related to the display, cursor control, parse tree modification, or parsing. Each of these areas will be discussed in turn below. Another group of editor routines provides interaction between the editor and the interpreter. These debugging routines will be the topic of the next section.

Display Routines

The AL editor supports two classes of display terminals: smart and dumb ones. A smart terminal is one that allows line insert and delete, along with character insert and delete within a line. This means the screen need not be redrawn explicitly by AL when, for example, a blank line is inserted in the middle of the display window; the terminal's hardware shifts the display appropriately. A dumb terminal is one where AL needs to explicitly redraw the screen. In either case the terminal must be cursor addressable.

A special display buffer is used to hold the characters being displayed. This display buffer consists of a character array. Routines to allocate a block of contiguous characters for a line, and to later release them, are part of the editor. A simple first-fit allocation algorithm is used. The first 150 characters of the buffer are reserved for use by the expression editor (described below).

Low-level support routines. To provide the necessary control over the terminal's display screen, the editor makes use of a number of low-level routines. These routines deal with necessary calls on the operating system and with the various peculiarities of the possible types of terminals. The routines are written in assembly language.

Before any display operations are performed, it is necessary to call an initialization routine which clears the screen and sets things up, e.g. turns off echoing, prepares for character by character input, etc. Passed to the initialization routine is the address of the display buffer array. The routine returns information to the editor describing the terminal currently being used: whether it is a smart or dumb terminal and how many lines fit on the screen.

There are several routines to affect the display. The basic output routine writes out a string of characters from the display buffer array to the screen starting at a given line and column. Another routine is used to write out a single character to any line/column position on the screen. This routine also has a boolean parameter specifying whether the character should be displayed in boldface. For smart terminals there are routines to insert and delete a given number of lines on the screen, and also to insert or delete a given number of characters in a line on the screen.

Another routine exists to display the terminal's cursor at any position on the screen. Other routines clear the screen and beep the terminal.

Two routines read characters typed by the user. The first waits for a character to be typed and returns it. This is the normal method; however, when the interpreter is running, a second routine is used. This other routine looks to see whether a character has been typed, and, if so, returns it; otherwise it returns immediately and indicates that no characters have been typed.

Finally, a routine exists to catch interrupts generated by ↑C (or some other break character[1]). The routine sets a boolean flag so that the interpreter can detect that the user wishes to interrupt program execution.

Echo window. At the bottom of the screen is the region where commands are echoed, system messages are displayed, and output from a running user AL program is printed. The echo window consists of two parts: the line currently being written into and those lines previously written. A character array is used to hold the line currently being written. When the line is completed by a carriage return, space is allocated from the display array for it, the characters in the line are copied into the display array, and a new line record is allocated to point to it. An array is used to point to these line records. When the last line in the echo window is reached, the region is shifted up a line and the previous top line is released.

Auxiliary routines exist to write one or several characters into the current echo line, to write an integer or real number out, and to delete the last character written.[2] When characters are written into the array holding the current echo line, they are not automatically displayed on the screen. The characters are written onto the display screen either when the entire line has been entered into the buffer—that is, a carriage return has completed the line—or when an auxiliary routine forces any characters in the current line not previously displayed to be written out.

Program display window. The majority of the display screen is used for the window into the user's current AL program. The routines to manipulate this window will be discussed in this subsection; those routines that convert from the internal parse tree representation to the "prettyprinted" characters shown on the display will be described in the next subsection.

As with the command echo region, the text in the current display window is stored in the display character array, and each line of the display has a line record associated with it. The editor maintains an array which points to these line records. Unless the program is very short, only part of it is stored in textual form. As the user moves the window in the program, old lines that are moved off the display screen are released and their space in the display array reclaimed. Actually, the editor will keep the textual form of those lines which are moved just off screen: the array of line records is approximately ten lines larger than the terminal's screen size. Thus, if the user shifts the display window back with, for example, a ↑B or a ↑T, to see what had just been moved off screen, the old lines will still be available and will not need to be recomputed. The array of lines in the program is described by three variables specifying the lines in the program associated with the top and bottom lines of the array and the offset into the array of the top line on the display screen.

One main routine is used to adjust the display window. It is given as an argument the line of the program to display at the top of the screen. If there would not be enough lines between the given one and the end of the program to fill the display window, then the argument is adjusted to bring in enough to do so. Then the new window into the program is checked to see if there is any overlap with those lines currently written in the display array. If so, the display and array of line records are rolled up or down appropriately, and any lines shifted out of the array are released. Otherwise, the entire old display is flushed. In any event, the prettyprinter routine, described below, is invoked to fill in the new lines for the display. If necessary, the cursor is reset and the new cursor position is displayed.

Another routine is used to make room for new lines on the display. It is passed arguments describing where in the program the new lines are to be inserted and how many of them there are. If any of the new lines are on the display screen, then blank lines are inserted in the appropriate place, and the following lines shifted down. Finally, the information on the header and trailer lines is updated.

A final routine is used to delete lines from the display. In the normal case, after deleting the lines requested, the lines following them are rolled up and new lines added, if necessary, to fill up the bottom of the screen via the prettyprint routine. If the remainder of the program after the deleted section is insufficient to fill out the display, then lines from the preceding part of the program are rolled down.

Both the insertion and deletion routines also adjust the position of user-placed marks and maintain the information in the cursor stack, described below.

Various other miscellaneous display-related routines exist to do such things as print out the header and trailer lines and redraw the entire display screen.

Prettyprinter. One of the major routines used by the editor is the prettyprinter. Given a pointer to the internal program representation, it produces a properly formatted textual representation of the program. While the primary use of the prettyprinter is for displaying the program on the screen, it is also used to set up the parse tree for the editor, to set the editor's cursor, and to locate statements in the parse tree, all of which are discussed below.

As mentioned above, the prettyprinter routine produces a textual representation of the program given the parse tree. It does this in a recursive manner, printing out the text for the current statement, calling itself when necessary to deal with any nested statements. In doing so, it makes use of several auxiliary routines that handle the printing of expressions, motion clauses, and lists of variable declarations.

As is the case with the command echo region, a character array is used to hold the line currently being written. When the line is completed by a carriage return, space is allocated in the display array for it, the characters are copied into it, a new line record is allocated to point to them, a pointer to the new line record is entered in the appropriate place in the main display window's line array, and, finally, the new line is displayed on the screen. When the line is written out to the display, only the first eighty characters will be shown; only when the line is being edited will the remaining characters be displayed on the following line.

There are a number of auxiliary routines to write into the character array for a new line. These include routines to write a single character, several characters, an integer, a real number, a vector, a transform, a string, or the list of tokens associated with a macro.

Normally, the prettyprinter is invoked when the display is shifted and several new lines must be added at the top or bottom of the screen. Two variables are used to specify the first and last new lines that need to be displayed. By using the field associated with each statement record that tells the number of lines required to print it, the prettyprinter can quickly determine which statements fall within the requested region and only print the relevant portions of them. A third variable indicating the line currently being prettyprinted is also used.

As mentioned above, the prettyprinter routine is also used to perform a number of other functions. Just after a program has been read in from a file, the field in each statement record that specifies the length of that statement in lines is filled in. A length field is also associated with all the expressions in the program, and these, too, need to be set up. A special boolean variable is used to indicate that the parse tree needs to be set up and the prettyprinter routine then called.

When the user wishes to write the program out to a file with the SAVE command, another special boolean variable is set and the prettyprinter is invoked. Instead of storing the lines of the program in the display array, they are written out to the specified file.

Another use of the prettyprinter routine is to locate a statement in the program. That is, given a pointer to a statement, locate it in the parse tree and determine what line it starts on. This is primarily used in conjunction with the TRACE command.

Finally, the prettyprinter is also used to set the editor's cursor to the current statement. More will be said about this below in the discussion of cursor control.

Line editor. When the user is typing an extended command, inserting a statement or clause, or modifying part of the program, the line editor is used. It enables the user to enter and modify a line of text, which is then processed by the editor. The user may start with a blank line or with text preloaded by the editor. The entire line may be modifiable or only a part of it. As described in the previous chapter, the line editor permits the user to move the cursor back and forth, inserting, deleting and modifying the text as desired.

The line editor is called with several parameters. The first specifies which line on the screen to place the line being edited. The next two indicate where in the display array the line to be edited starts and how long it is. Another two parameters designate the location in the line where the part to be edited starts and how long it initially is. A final parameter is used to specify where in this part the cursor should initially be placed.

The first thing the line editor routine does is to copy the line being edited into space reserved for line editing at the beginning of the display array. If the line exceeds eighty characters, then the overflow characters are displayed on the following line. Hardware permitting, the part of the line being edited is displayed in boldface.

The line editor then goes into its basic command loop: waiting for the user to type a character and then processing it. If the character typed is an ASCII control character, it is interpreted as a line editor command. The line editor commands either move the cursor, delete characters from the array, recopy the original line into the array, cause the line editor to enter insert mode, or exit the line editor. Regular characters will either overwrite the character in the line editor array at the current cursor position, or, in insert mode, be inserted into the array there with all the following characters in the array shifted over one place.

When the user types a non-line editor command, then the line editor will exit and the edited line will then be processed. Before returning, the line editor restores the following line if the edited line had overflowed onto it. Various global variables are set up so the statement editor is ready to parse the edited line. Finally, the line editor returns control back to the statement editor, passing back the control character that terminated the line editor along with the new length of the edited part of the line.

Cursor Control

When modifying or simply moving about in the user's AL program, the editor needs to know the context of the current cursor position. This includes both the position in the parse tree of the statement or clause the cursor is currently pointing to, and the positions of those statements that surround it. This information is contained in an array of cursor records, organized as a stack. The topmost record describes the cursor's position, the next record describes the statement that the cursor is nested in, and so on, down to the bottom two records which point to the outermost block of the program and the special program statement record. A special routine to print out the cursor array proved quite useful during the development and debugging of the editor. The routine was invoked with an unused control character: ↑Y.

As mentioned above, the prettyprinter routines are used to set up this cursor stack. As each statement or clause is printed, a check is made to see whether it encloses the line that the cursor is pointing to, and, if so, a cursor record pointing to it is pushed on the cursor array.

To move the cursor by a given number of lines, as would be the case with the editor commands—⟨cr⟩, ⟨bs⟩, <, >, ↑W, and ↑U—the number of lines being moved is added to or subtracted from the current cursor line to determine the new cursor line, and the new cursor position set with the prettyprinter routine. For the editor commands—↑L, ↑O, ↑G, and @—the new cursor line is set directly and the prettyprinter routine is invoked.

For those editor commands—↑S, ↑N, and ↑—which move the cursor according to the program's lexical structure, special routines are used. Moving to the parent statement with ↑ is simple—all that needs to be done is pop the current cursor record from the cursor stack, leaving the parent statement's cursor record on top. Two other routines exist to move down or up a statement in the parse tree. They each take two arguments: the number of statements to move and whether to stay at the same lexical level or descend into any subtrees.

To keep track of the lines that have been marked with the extended MARK command, an integer array containing the line numbers of the marked lines is used. The line numbers are stored in ascending order. When a line is marked, its line number in the program is inserted into the marks array in the appropriate place. The marks array is updated whenever lines are inserted or deleted in the program, so that the mark stays attached to the correct line. Two steps are required to move to a marked line. First the marks array is searched to locate where the cursor is relative to the various marked lines. Then the appropriate entry can be located and the cursor and display shifted to it.

Parse Tree Modification

The main function of the editor is, of course, to edit the program. This means modifying the program's parse tree. Possible modifications include changing an existing statement or clause, inserting a new one, or deleting an old one.[3] Each of these will be discussed in turn. However, the translation from the characters entered to the internal representation, that is, the actual parsing methods used, will first be described.

Parsing methods. The AL system currently makes use of two distinct parsers. The first version of the system consisted of the interpreter and a recursive descent parser. It was written to provide an initial means of testing out the new arm servo module while the full interactive AL system was being developed. It also was used to develop and debug the interpreter. The parser for this early system was designed to read in a previously written file containing an AL program or a program typed in at the terminal. No provisions were made for interacting with the user or allowing editing of the program.

As the editing and debugging facilities were added to the system, an incremental parser was added. Where recursive descent parser treats the parsing of a complete statement, including any statements nested in it, as an atomic operation, the incremental one is geared towards parsing, at one time, only that part of a statement that fits on a single line. The problem of extraneous errors being generated during incremental parsing is avoided by only allowing the user to edit syntactically correct subtrees.

The incremental parser shares many of the routines used by the recursive descent parser, some involving minor changes. The incremental parser is used when inserting a new statement or when modifying an old one. The recursive descent parser is still used when reading in a program from a file with the GET command and also for immediate statements. Eventually the incremental parser will be extended to handle these functions too, and the recursive descent parser will be eliminated.[4] The rest of this section will describe routines common to both parsers. Their differences will be noted.

When a line is either entered with the line editor or read in from a file, the characters in it must be parsed and translated into the internal representation used by the AL system. The first step in this process is to break the input into lexical tokens. This is done by a routine that, when called, will return the next token in the line. The possible token types which are recognized include reserved words, identifiers, labels, delimiting characters, real numbers, strings, and comments. Two auxiliary routines are used to look up reserved words and identifiers by searching the appropriate hashed list. A special delimiter is used to indicate the end of the line for the incremental parser.

During the parsing of the program, there are certain situations where comments will be ignored and not become part of the parse tree, for example, inside arithmetic expressions. A global flag determines whether the next token routine will return comments or flush any it encounters and instead return the next non-comment token.

The routine that gets the next token also expands macros. When an identifier is read in that is the name of a macro, several things happen. First, any arguments are bound to the macro's formal parameters. If another macro was in the process of being expanded, then its state is saved in a special macro stack. A pointer to the current macro is then pushed on another stack. Finally, the first token of the macro is returned.[5] A similar process occurs when a formal macro parameter is seen.

Each token in a macro body, or actual macro argument, has a pointer to the next token in the expansion. After returning the last token, this pointer is nil and when the next token is requested, the completed macro will be popped from the macro stack and the state of the previous macro, if any, will be restored.

Another routine is used to parse arithmetic expressions. This is done using a straightforward operator precedence scheme. Two stacks, one for operators and one for operands, are built up out of node records. A third integer array is used to hold the associated operator precedences. Several auxiliary routines are used to push and pop values on these stacks, look up variables, perform type and dimension checking, etc. When parsing an expression, all tokens up to the next reserved word or delimiter are processed.

The basic arithmetic operators— $+$, $-$, $*$, and $/$—are used in several different contexts. For example, $+$ can be used to add two reals, two vectors, or a vector offset to a frame.

When parsing an expression, a check is made that the data types of the various operands agree with those required by the operators. If an error occurs, an appropriate error message is printed and a special node record inserted in the expression tree to mark the expression as being bad. This "bad" node contains a pointer to the part of the expression that is in error, so it can be printed and edited later. Another pointer points to a leaf node of the expected data type. A check is also made that the physical dimensions of the operands and resulting expressions match. If not, an error message will be displayed.

When an identifier is encountered while parsing an expression, a search is made to bind it to the correct variable definition. This search consists of running down the list of variables associated with each of the blocks and procedures surrounding the current line until one is found that points to the correct identifier record.[6] For the incremental parser, the cursor stack contains pointers to all the surrounding blocks and procedures. For the recursive descent parser, two global variables point to the current block and the current procedure, if any. Each of these in turn has back pointers to any surrounding blocks or procedures. This simple lookup scheme is sufficient, since AL programs tend to have a small (several dozen) number of variables.

If no associated variable record is found when attempting to bind an identifier, then a new variable will be created and added to the variable list of either the block of the innermost surrounding procedure definition or the outermost block of the program, if there is no such surrounding procedure. An error message will be printed telling the user that this is being done. A special pointer is then set to the newly created declaration statement. At the conclusion of the current statement, the new declaration statement will be spliced into the appropriate block and the display will be updated. When the new variable is created, no data type is associated with it, but an attempt will be made to determine a unique data type when the context surrounding it is parsed. For example, scalars can only be added to scalars, or the left side of an assignment statement must be the same type as the right side expression. If no such determination can be made, the variable's type will be undefined, until the user edits the declaration statement.[7]

Whenever a new variable is declared, or an old one is modified or deleted, there may be changes in the lexical scoping of the variables within the block or procedure containing the declaration statement. When such a change occurs, all of the expressions in the affected block are reparsed to maintain the program's integrity. This reparsing is done by running through the statements in the block, taking each expression in them in turn, and converting it to a textual representation, which is then passed to the expression parser. The reparsed expression is stored back in the corresponding statement. If any variables have become undeclared, then an error message will be generated, and new declaration statements for them will be added. Note that unless there is a more global declaration of a variable, it is impossible to delete it until all uses of the variable have been removed, since the system will automatically add it back again.

Besides the need to reparse whenever a variable is created, deleted, or changed, the interpreter's environment will also need to be updated if the change occurs in an active block. The editor will alter the appropriate process's environment record to include, delete or modify the correct environment entry record for the variable.

Insertions. The basic way that new statements and clauses are inserted into the user's AL program is with the ↑I command. This causes the editor to insert a blank line on the screen at the line the cursor is pointing to. The line editor is then positioned at this blank line and the user may enter the new statement or clause. The incremental parser is then used to translate it. The first token of the line, taken with the context where the insertion is being made, is sufficient to determine what type of statement or clause[8] is being added. The editor then creates a new statement or clause record of the correct type. The parser will try to fill in the various fields associated with it by reading in the rest of the line. Any required fields that are not explicitly specified will be given a default value.[9] Finally, the new statement or clause is properly formatted with the prettyprinter routine and redrawn. If the end of the line of input had not been reached, then the insertion routine will repeat the above steps using the remainder of the previously entered line.

The last step in parsing any statement is to set up the evaluation ordering of all the expressions associated with the statement. A routine to do this is passed a pointer to each expression tree in turn, along with a pointer to the current head node of the evaluation ordering list. The routine then recursively traverses the expression tree in preorder, threading the nodes of the expression for the interpreter. A final parameter passed to the routine specifies whether constants are to be pushed onto the stack, as would be the case for subscripts, or left for the interpreter to explicitly look up. The routine then returns the new head node for the evaluation order list, which is stored in a field of the statement record. For motion statements, another routine is invoked which runs through all of the clauses associated with the motion, calling the evaluation ordering routine for each of them.

When the user types ↑I, the editor first checks that an insertion would be legal at the current cursor position. For example, no insertions are valid if the cursor is pointing to the ELSE clause of an IF statement, or to the first statement in the body of any loop statement. If an insertion would not be legal, an error message is printed; otherwise the user is allowed to enter the insertion with the line editor. Before the input line is parsed, the editor checks the current cursor context to determine whether either a new statement or motion clause or both is allowable. If the user's input is not valid in the current context, it will be ignored and an error message will be printed.

Another way that a statement may be inserted into the user's program is by entering a statement for immediate execution when collect mode has been enabled. The statement will have been parsed by the recursive descent parser using as many lines of input, via the line editor, as are necessary to enter the text for the entire statement. The new statement is then spliced into the program at the current cursor location. The prettyprinter routine is used to format and display the statement before it is executed. If the cursor does not point to the beginning of a statement in a BEGIN-END block, then an error messsage will be printed and collect mode will be disabled.

A third way to add a new statement to the program is with the DEFINE command, which will add a new assignment statement for each variable specified by the user. The editor first obtains the variable's current value from the interpreter and then creates a new assignment statement that will assign the variable that current value. This new statement is then spliced into the program. The same constraints mentioned for collect mode above apply to the cursor's position; otherwise an error message is displayed.

The "[" command provides a final way to insert a new statement into the parse tree. In this case, the cursor must be pointing at a statement which will be surrounded by a new BEGIN-END block. The new block is spliced into the parse tree where the statement formerly was.

When an insertion of any of the above types takes place, each parent statement that encloses the newly inserted statement must also be updated. The field specifying the number of lines taken up in the display by the parent statement must be incremented by the number of lines just added. Also, any entries in the mark table for lines that follow the inserted line must be shifted down by the number of lines just inserted to keep them with the lines that they mark.

Changes. Once a statement or clause has been added to the user's AL program, it may be subsequently modified by pointing the cursor at it and typing a ⟨space⟩. The editor will load the line editor with the line, opening any expressions in it for the user to change. The old expressions will be released. Keywords such as IF, FOR, and MOVE will not be modifiable, so the user will not be able to change the basic statement or clause type. After the user has made any desired changes in the line, it will be reparsed with the incremental parser. The evaluation order list of expressions associated with the statement will then be recomputed. Finally, the display will be updated by the prettyprinter. This may require that statements such as PRINT or AFFIX be reformatted to take up one more or one less line.

AFFIX statements may also be modified by pointing the cursor at the statement and using the AT command. The editor will then get the current values from the interpreter of the two frames affixed by the statement. The resulting values will be used to compute the spatial transformation between the two frames by

$$f_1 * INV (f_2)$$

where f_1 is being affixed to f_2. Either a new AT phrase will be added to the statement, or the old one will be modified, to remember this transform's value.

Deletions. The ↑D command causes the editor to delete one or more subtrees from the parse tree. Only subtrees of the same kind and at the same lexical level in the program will be deleted in the same operation. At one time the user can delete several clauses from a motion statement or several statements in a list. If, when deleting a statement, that statement had been the body of a loop, or the THEN part of an IF statement, then an empty statement will be inserted in its place. An END statement cannot be deleted: the block as a whole must be deleted by pointing at the appropriate BEGIN statement. The same is true for a COEND statement.

When a statement is deleted, any processes that are currently executing the deleted statement are reset to continue execution with the next statement in the program.[10] Any marks that had been set inside the statement are also shifted to point to the next undeleted line.

The entire program is deleted and its space reclaimed when a GET command is issued. The new program is read in with the recursive descent parser, and all of the variables in its outermost block are initialized by the interpreter.

4.5 Debugger

This section will examine the debugging facilities that connect the user, through the editor, to the interpreter. A debugging routine is invoked whenever a user command requires an action by the interpreter. The section starts off by describing how the system keeps track of the processes at various debugging levels. Then the routines to show and change the debugging context are discussed. The section concludes with a description of the routines used to alter the program's control flow and to perform immediate execution.

Debugging   ls

Initially, there is one process associated with the user's AL program. As the program is executed, it may sprout other processes to handle condition monitors and coblocks. At any time the user can suspend execution of this tree of processes and initiate a new process to execute an immediate statement. This new process may also sprout auxiliary processes and may be suspended in turn. To keep track of which processes are suspended and which the interpreter should execute, a field in each process descriptor block specifies the debugging level that the process is running at. When the debugger passes control to the interpreter, the current debugging level is also passed. The interpreter will only run processes at the debugging level.

An array of pointers is used to keep track of the process descriptor block associated with each immediately executing statement. Any processes it may sprout will be kept on the interpreter's list of current processes.

The debugging level is incremented by one whenever a new statement is entered for immediate execution. It is decremented by one when the process associated with that statement terminates or when the user flushes it with the POP command. All the processes at the old debugging level are then terminated and their process descriptor blocks released.

The Current Context

At any time during the course of the program development session, many different processes may be active, and they are apt to be running at various debugging levels. The TRACE ALL command will display the procedure-call chains for every process which is currently in use. The processes are listed according to their debugging levels: first the current immediate statements and last the actual program execution. Each process has its status reported, which includes both which queue it is in, and where in the program it is. A process may be running, waiting to run, waiting for input, waiting for an event, waiting for a force-sensing condition to occur, sleeping, waiting for processes it has sprouted to join, or waiting for a motion to finish. The position of the process in the program is described by the line number of the statement that it is currently executing. The line number is contained in the process's pdb, and it is set whenever the interpreter returns control to the debugger. This number is prefaced by either the word MAIN, if the statement is in the body of the main program, or by the name of the procedure containing the statement. A boolean field in each pdb indicates whether it is a procedure or not, and, if so, contains a pointer to the procedure's definition—which, in turn, has a pointer to the procedure's name. For procedures, the location from which they were called is also reported all the way up the call chain to the main program. A pointer in the pdb of the process associated with each procedure points to the caller. Processes associated with a condition monitor are indicated by another field in the pdb and are prefaced with (cmon). For immediately executed statements, the location is denoted by (tty:)/***.

Of these many processes, one is singled out to provide the context for debugger operations. This process is selected by using the editor to position the cursor in it. The routine that determines the current context looks for the process running at the highest debugging level that surrounds the current cursor position. This is done by searching for a process whose defining statement is the same as one of the surrounding statements pointed to by one of the entries in the current cursor stack. The search is conducted by checking all the processes at one debugging level against each entry in the cursor stack, and if none are satisfactory then the next lower debugging level is checked. For the sorts of AL programs that have been developed in the past, this method will practically always select the proper process. Failures should occur only if several instances of a recursive procedure were active.[11] Even in this case there is a good chance the right process would be selected, but if not, two commands are designed to explicitly select the correct process. The SET LEX i command would move up the procedure call stack to the *i*th procedure while the SET CONTEXT n command would selected the nth process, as numbered by the TRACE ALL command. Neither of these commands has yet been implemented.

The user can request that the top debugging level be immediately terminated, and that the previous debugging level be made active again, with the POP command. If the lowest debugging level, the one associated with the running program, is popped, then the variables declared in any inner blocks are flushed. The environment associated with the outermost block of the program is not currently affected by this command, though in the future, the user will be given the choice of zeroing all these global variables if desired.

Altering Control Flow

The debugger gives the user control over the order in which the statements in the program are executed. This control includes the ability to stop when a certain point is reached, i.e. setting breakpoints, to single step to the next statement, to execute an arbitrary statement next, etc. The implementation of these facilities will be described below.

All of the debugger facilities use one common routine to invoke the interpreter. Before passing control to the interpreter, it first calls an auxiliary routine to flush any old processes left over from the previous immediate statement execution, i.e. any processes sprouted at a higher debugging level than the current one. The interpreter is then called, and it commences program execution with the process indicated as being currently active. Eventually, it returns control back to the debugging routine which will report to the user if a breakpoint has been encountered or if the end of the program has been reached. If any immediate statements are still active, the current debugging level is also shown. Also, if an immediate statement has finished, then the associated process is terminated and the debugging level decreased by one. Next, any temporary breakpoints set for single stepping are cleared. Then the prettyprinter routine is used to set the cursor to the statement that the interpreter will execute next. Finally, for each process that is running, the prettyprinter routine is used to set the field in its pdb indicating the line number in the program of the statement that the process will execute next.

In the following discussion, any time a debugging routine "invokes the interpreter," it does so using the above routine. Prior to calling it, it is sometimes necessary to swap in a new process so that process can be executed. This is done by another auxiliary routine. It first will remove the process from any other queue it may be a member of. The previously running process will then be swapped out to the list of active processes. If no process is specified to be swapped in, and there is no currently running process, then the process heading the active list is swapped in. This last is the case after an immediate statement has finished being executed and its associated process has been flushed; the process which had last been running at the previous lower debugging level is then made active.

When the START command is given, all processes are flushed except the one associated with the main program,[12] and all the environments are unwound to the outermost block: that is, all but the variables in the outermost block are flushed. The main program's process is reset to commence execution with the first statement of the program, it is swapped in, and, finally, the above mentioned routine is called to invoke the interpreter.

The PROCEED command results in the interpreter being invoked to continue execution of the process it had last been running.

Breakpoints. Each statement record has a boolean field used to indicate a breakpoint being set at the statement. Whenever the interpreter encounters a statement with this field set to true, it will break and return control to the editor/debugger. Breakpoints are either set explicitly by the user with the BREAK command, or implicitly when single stepping. A breakpoint set implicitly is referred to as a temporary breakpoint, since it will be cleared after the debugging operation which set it is finished.

Two arrays are used to keep track of the regular and temporary breakpoints which are set at any given time. Each entry in the arrays points to a statement that has a breakpoint currently set. One array is used for temporary breakpoints, and the other for explicitly set ones. Whenever a breakpoint is set, an entry is made in the appropriate array and the break field in the statement record set to true. When a request to clear a regular breakpoint is made with the UNBREAK command, the statement's break field is checked and, if it is indeed set, then it is cleared and the regular breakpoint array searched for the corresponding entry, which is then removed.

Two routines exist to clear all of the breakpoints of each type. When the user issues the UNBREAK ALL command, each statement listed in the regular breakpoint array has its break flag cleared, and the array is zeroed. The array of temporary breakpoints is cleared whenever the interpreter returns control to the editor/debugger.

Single stepping. Two routines provide a singe-stepping capability. They set temporary breakpoints in the parse tree based on where the next statement to be executed by the currently selected process can transfer control. The user can request four different degrees of single stepping based on the lexical structure of the program. Two routines handle the setting of the required temporary breakpoints.

The first of these is an auxiliary routine which is passed a statement and sets a temporary breakpoint at it, unless it is an END statement. In that case, breakpoints are set at the parent of the END statement, and at the statement following the parent. If the END statement is not just marking the end of a list of statements, but is actually in the program, a breakpoint is also set at it.

The second, and main, routine is passed an integer indicating the level of single stepping desired. In order of increasing step size, these levels are: (1) step to the next statement this process will execute, including procedure calls; (2) is the same as (1), but excluding procedure calls; (3) step to the next statement at the same lexical level; and (4) step up to the next statement at a greater lexical level. The first three of these levels form a proper subset and are handled together, while the last is treated separately. The statement being stepped from is determined by checking the pdb of the currently selected process to see what statement it will execute next.

For level (1) above, the list of expressions needed by that statement is searched for the first procedure call in it. If one is found then a temporary breakpoint is placed at the first statement in the body of the procedure. For levels (1) and (2), a check is made if the statement has any other statements nested inside it. If so, then a breakpoint is set at each nested statement it can branch to, e.g. the body of a loop, or the THEN and ELSE parts of an IF statement. For levels (1), (2) and (3), a breakpoint is set at the following statement using the auxiliary routine described above, which will handle the case where the next statement is at a higher lexical level. If the statement is a RETURN, then a breakpoint will be set at the statement which follows the one that called the procedure, again using the auxiliary routine. Further, if level (1) stepping is being done, then the remaining expression list of the calling statement is checked for another procedure call, and if there is one, a breakpoint will be placed at the first statement in its body.

When stepping up a level—that is, type (4)—the routine runs through the list of statements at the current lexical level until it reaches the end of the list. The auxiliary routine is then called to set a breakpoint at the parent statement and its successor. If the current statement is inside a procedure, then an additional breakpoint is set at the statement following the call to the procedure.

After placing the appropriate temporary breakpoints, the interpreter will be invoked. When it next returns control back to the editor/debugger, all of the temporary breakpoints will be cleared.

Currently, only one process at a time is single stepped; the other processes are executed until they block naturally. At some point an extended command, SET STEP ON, will be implemented to provide a facility to single step all processes.

It will set a global flag for the interpreter which will cause it to break back to the editor/debugger after it executes each statement. The command, SET STEP OFF, will clear the flag and cause the interpreter to resume normal program execution.

Related to single stepping is the TSTEP command. It causes a temporary breakpoint to be set at the statement the cursor is pointing to currently. The interpreter is then started up. When it returns control, the breakpoint will be cleared.

GO. the GO command causes the currently selected process to next execute the statement pointed to by the current cursor. This is done by changing the statement pointer in the process's pdb, along with resetting the expression pointer and the mode field. If, prior to issuing the GO, the process had been inside any inner blocks and the GO will cause it to exit these blocks, then any environments associated with those blocks are unwound. Likewise, any processes which may have been sprouted in them are flushed.

Next, a check is made to determine whether the GO is jumping into a thread of a coblock which is not already active—that is, whether a statement that would normally be run in parallel with several others inside of a COBEGIN-COEND block is now going to be run by itself. If this is the case then a temporary form of nowait mode is automatically enabled. When the command SET NOWAIT ON is given, a flag in the interpreter is set. It will remain set until either the user explicitly clears it with a SET NOWAIT OFF or SET WAIT ON command, or until a START command restarts the program execution. When nowait mode is entered implicitly by jumping into a thread of a coblock statement, the debugger makes a note of the process's current debugging level. If the actual debugging level ever becomes less that that, then nowait mode will be cleared. It should also be mentioned that when the interpreter finishes executing the thread it will notice that the thread had not been sprouted as a parallel process, and will break back to the debugger.

Finally, the debugging level is set to that of the selected process, so any processes associated with immediate statements at a greater debugging level will be aborted. The selected process is then swapped in and the interpreter invoked.

Immediate execution. When a statement is entered for immediate execution, a new process will be created to run it, and the debugging level will be incremented by one. The new process will be set up to use the current environment. That is, the pdb pointer to the current process's environment header is copied to the pdb of the new process.

To identify immediate statements so that the interpreter will return control after executing them, and so that the space they occupy can eventually be released, they are followed by an ABORT statement. The ABORT statement has an integer field which is used to hold the debugging level associated with the abort. If this field is greater than zero, then the ABORT statement is treated specially. When the interpreter encounters it, if the debugging level associated with the ABORT statement is less than the current debugging level, it will be ignored. If it is the same, then control is passed back to the debugger which then releases the immediate statement, along with the ABORT statement, and decrements the debugging level by one.

When collect mode is set, any statement entered for immediate execution is first added to the user's AL program. An ABORT statement is then spliced into the actual program following the statement. After the statement is executed, the ABORT statement will be removed. This is also the case when a statement in the program is immediately executed using the EXECUTE command.

To immediately execute a statement, a debugging routine is called with a pointer to the statement to be executed. This routine increments the debugging level, sets up a new process, appends an ABORT statement, swaps in the new process, and, finally, invokes the interpreter to execute it.

The interpreter treats RETURN and ABORT statements slightly differently during immediate execution. When a RETURN statement is encountered, a check is made to see whether it is being executed by a process associated with an immediately executed statement. This check involves several fields in the process's pdb. If it is an immediately executed RETURN statement, then the return is from the currently selected process at the next lower debugging level and not from the currently executing process. The interpreter causes the interrupted process to return from whatever procedure it was in. Control is then passed back to the editor/debugger. The way ABORT statements are handled has already been described.

Whenever an expression is entered for immediate evaluation another routine creates a new PRINT statement to pass to the interpreter to compute the expression and display the results. This statement is then passed to the above-mentioned routine which sets up a new process and invokes the interpreter.

4.6 Force Graphics Subsystem

This section describes the GAL force graphics module, which is part of the old AL system. The old AL system has been described elsewhere [Binford et al. 1975, 1976, 1977], but a brief summary of the salient features is provided below. This is followed by a discussion of how the GAL module interfaces to it.

Old AL System

The old AL system involved two separate computers. A large main frame, SAIL's DEC KL10, was used to edit and compile the user's programs. The compiled program would then be downloaded to a minicomputer, a PDP-11/45, which would run the program and actually control the arms. The two machines were connected by an interface (called the ELF interface) which allowed the large machine read/write access to the smaller machine's memory.

The output from the compiler was code for an "AL machine," which would be emulated on the PDP-11/45 by the AL runtime system. This runtime system consisted of two main modules: an AL interpreter and an arm servo, which have become the two processes that make up the new interactive AL system.

The AL compiler was written in SAIL, an ALGOL dialect. The runtime system was written in PDP-11 assembly code.

GAL Interface to Old AL System

Since there were no graphic terminals connected to the PDP-11/45 it was necessary to make use of the Data Disk terminals on SAIL to display the force data. This meant that a program on the DEC KL10 would be running in parallel to the AL runtime system on the PDP-11/45. This program, called GAL, would then communicate with AL. Any gathered force data would be passed over to it, and the user could then display the various force components.

This interprocess communication was done by using three words in the PDP-11/45's memory as mailboxes. The AL runtime system, on the PDP-11/45, could directly access them, while GAL, on the DEC KL10, could get at them via the ELF interface. The first of these dedicated locations is used to indicate that the GAL module is present. This word is initially zeroed when the AL runtime system is loaded, and will be set by GAL when it starts up. If this word is not set, then any gather requests in the user's AL program will be ignored. The second location is used to contain a pointer to the force data buffer. If it is zero then there is no data for GAL to read. A non-zero value tells GAL where to find the force data from the previous motion. The force buffer pointed to is prefaced by two words which indicate which force components were gathered, and how many data points there are. The third word is a flag, indicating when it is set, that the data is valid, i.e. that the gathering motion has finished.

After force data for a motion has been collected and read in by GAL, the user has a choice as to whether the AL program should proceed until it reaches the next motion statement or the next motion that will gather more force data, or whether it should just continue running, overwriting any old force data when a gathering motion is executed. This interlocking between GAL and the running AL program is indicated by two words specifying the buffer pointer and the data valid flag.

The AL runtime system checks before each motion that at least one of the two words is zero. If both are non-zero, then the runtime system will sleep until one of them becomes zero. A check is also made before each gathering motion that the buffer pointer has been zeroed, and, if not, the system again will wait until it has been. So, if the user had specified that AL should wait when the next motion statement is encountered, then GAL will not zero the two words until the Continue command is given. If pauses are desired only for gathering motions, then GAL will clear the data valid flag after the force data has been read in, but will wait for a Continue command before zeroing the buffer pointer. Finally, if no waiting is desired, then as soon as GAL finishes reading in the force data it will zero both words.

A typical sequence of operations would then be as follows. The AL runtime system is loaded and started. GAL is later started and sets the flag word indicating that it is present to the runtime system. At this point, GAL goes into a wait loop, both checking for user commands, and also examining the buffer pointer and data valid flag to see whether force data is ready to be fetched. When a gathering motion is encountered in the user's AL program, the runtime system first clears the data valid flag and sets the buffer pointer word to the starting address of where the force data will be written. At the conclusion of the motion, the data valid flag will be set, causing GAL to awaken, and the runtime system will continue executing the program. GAL will then read in the buffer pointer word to locate the data buffer for this motion. The two words are then read that specify which force components are present and how many samples were taken. The raw data is then read in and converted from the floating point format used on the PDP-11/45 to that recognized by the DEC KL10. A message is then displayed to notify the user which force components had been read in. Depending on what form of motion interlock the user had previously specified, either both the buffer pointer and data valid flag are cleared (do not wait), just the data valid flag is cleared (wait before next gathering motion), or neither is cleared (wait for next motion). The runtime system will then continue executing the program accordingly. The user can now issue commands to display the force data. A command to continue with the next motion can also be given which will zero the two words, and, if the runtime system is waiting, it will proceed. Eventually the user may cause GAL to exit; when it does so it will clear the flag that had indicated that it was running.

Before concluding the description of GAL, mention should be made of its use as a top-level interface between the user and SAIL. To run a compiled AL program, it is necessary to first download the AL runtime system and then download the user's program. This downloading is done with an auxiliary program that runs on the DEC KL10. It reads in a file on the DEC KL10 and uses the ELF interface to write the file's contents into the PDP-11/45's memory. This auxiliary program has no special knowledge about AL, and the user had to learn a number of different commands to use the program. A command file existed to help insulate the user from this other program, but it was of limited utility.

One of the features of GAL was the ability to download both the AL runtime system and users' programs. Since GAL knew all about AL, it was much easier to use it than to use the more general auxiliary program mentioned above. So GAL was used even when no force displaying was to be done.

5

Conclusion

This chapter starts by reviewing the major problems that arise when writing a manipulator program. It then goes on to evaluate how well the designed manipulator programming environment aids the user in developing these manipulator programs. It concludes by mentioning some topics for future work.

5.1 Summary

In a nutshell, the fundamental problem of manipulator programming is to *fully* describe the motion of the objects being assembled, and to then translate this description into motions of the manipulators that perform the desired assembly operations. This involves specifying positions, velocities, forces applied and sensed, and other details. All told, there is an incredible amount of information that must be provided.

Hence, the fundamental task facing manipulator languages and manipulator programming systems is aiding the user in specifying this required information. Such a system has been described in the previous chapters. The following discussion will reiterate some of the specific problems and then point out how the interactive AL system helps to solve them.

Problems of Manipulator Programming

This section briefly repeats the problems that arise in writing a manipulator program, as discussed in chapter 2. A major point, which cannot be said too often, is that the entire process is a highly interactive one.

Each of the objects used in the assembly must be defined. This consists of specifying both the location of each object in the workspace and the position of any special features on the objects. This information is needed to provide the initial model of the manipulator's world for the assembly task. During the program development session it is also necessary to modify the model to reflect changes that have occurred in the physical world due to programming errors or user intervention.

As each motion sequence is written, it must be tested to check that it works as planned. This testing uncovers bugs which require modifications to the motions in the sequence. To confirm that the corrections work, the sequence must be retried, which first requires restoring the state to what it had been prior to executing the sequence.

Many motions will either apply or sense forces. The various force parameters in these motions need to be tuned. The user needs some form of feedback, preferably graphic, from the force system if this tuning is to be done intelligently.

When multiple arms or devices are used for assembly, it will usually be desired to have them operate concurrently. This makes it necessary to coordinate their activities.

How Interactive AL Helps

The interactive AL manipulator programming environment described in the previous two chapters was designed to solve the above mentioned problems. How well it does so will be discussed below.

The AL system provides a state-of-the-art programming environment for manipulator programming. As such it is highly interactive, allowing the user considerable flexibility in developing manipulator programs. The system has been written in Pascal for portability to other machines. The separation of the interpreter and the actual arm servos into separate tasks, which run concurrently and communicate via messages, is a step towards distributing the system over several computers.

Interpreter. To provide the necessary flexibility to the user when writing and debugging manipulator programs, the AL system makes use of an interpreter. By representing the program as a parse tree it is very easy for the user to make changes in it with the editor while debugging, without destroying any of the current context.

While use of a parse tree representation simplifies program editing and debugging, it does create a significant problem due to the space required to hold the parse tree. For some sample AL programs, the parse tree occupied approximately six times the space as was used to hold the same program in the old compiler-based AL system. Much of this is due to the increased space taken up by the expression subtrees. As a consequence, with the small address space available on the PDP-11/45, the current implementation is limited to small programs. This is a serious deficiency.

Usually interpreters are much slower than compiler-based systems, but for manipulator programs this is generally not the case. Program execution tends to be dominated by the time taken for arms to be moved; each arm motion may require from one to several seconds. Of course, it is important that the servo code be optimized, but this is part of the runtime system and is independent of the interpreter's operation.

The majority of arithmetic expressions evaluated during an AL program involve operations on *vectors* and *transes*, which are performed by compiled runtime routines—just as they would be in a compiler-based system. The AL programs written thus far have not been computationally intensive, so interpreting AL programs has not been significantly slower than running them compiled. If this changes in the future and manipulator programs become compute bound, then the use of an interpreter-based system may need to be reevaluated.

Editor. One of the main design goals for the editor has been to allow the user to easily modify the developing program. For the types of changes that are commonly made when debugging motion sequences, this has been fairly well achieved. Likewise, it is straightforward for the user to insert new statements and clauses into the program and to subsequently modify them.

One problem with the current implementation is that a sequence of statements that is currently part of some block in the program cannot be made into a procedure or placed in a loop. This is because the attach command has not yet been implemented. The problem will be solved when the ability to ATTACH statements and move them about is added to the editor. The current lack of a COPY command is also a minor shortcoming.

A more fundamental deficiency is that once a statement is inserted it is impossible to change it to another type of statement, for example changing a FOR loop to a WHILE loop. To make this type of change involves creating a new statement of the desired type, attaching the various subfields of the old statement and moving them to the new one, and finally deleting the old statement—which, while straightforward, is somewhat tedious. This is a common problem with all syntax-directed editors.

Another problem exists with regard to prettyprinting the user's program. The current implementation is quite rigid about how the program is to be formatted. While the resulting programs are quite readable, they could be made even clearer. The ability to add blank lines between distinct sections of the program would be a definite help, as would being able to place comments to the right of the statement they describe, instead of on the following or preceding line. Additional control to allow placing several short statements on one line or suppressing display of statements below a specified level would also be useful. Some systems vary the formatting automatically [Mikelsons 1981] while others require explicit user commands [Teitelbaum 1981].

The way the current implementation handles macros leaves something to be desired. By immediately expanding each macro call when it is parsed and not placing any mention of it into the parse tree, the editor is throwing away useful information. If the macro's definition is subsequently changed, there is no way of reflecting those changes in the program at each point that the macro was called. Likewise, when displaying the program, or storing it in a file, the user would generally like the editor to display the macro call and not its expansion. Macro calls could be easily added to the parse tree only if their expansion always resulted in a proper subtree.

Debugger. The use of the editor as the interface to the debugger, and hence the interpreter, is a major factor in the success of the current design. It is responsible for the ease with which a section of the program can be tried out, subsequently modified, and then retried. The standard debugging commands to set breakpoints, single step, etc. also aid in this program development.

Using the editor to set the context within which the debugging will occur is a very helpful feature not found in other systems. It allows the user to easily move around in the various environments that may be active at any given moment, examining and modifying the variables in them.

The debugger and editor also interact to the programmer's benefit by allowing statements entered for immediate execution to be inserted into the developing program (collect mode). The special commands, DEFINE and AT, aid the user in creating and modifying the models of the objects used in the program. Building these object models is also facilitated by being able to interactively control the various manipulators by executing any desired AL statements.

Some help is provided the user in dealing with the multiple processes that arise from concurrent use of multiple manipulators. Much more needs to be done here however. In particular, a special mode to single step all active processes would be useful. Likewise, a command is needed to allow the user to swap out the currently running process and swap in another. The use of no wait mode provides help in debugging an individual thread of a concurrent operation when it is run by itself.

The GO command allows the user to alter the control flow of a process directly. The process is immediately swapped in and run. A deferred version of the GO command is needed that will change which statement will next be executed by the process, but not start the process running. The statement would not be executed until the process is subsequently made active, for example, when the user issues a PROCEED command.

Force Graphics System. Finally, the force graphics subsystem of the old AL system greatly facilitates working with forces by making them visible and therefore accessible to the manipulator programmer.

5.2 Future Work

While the new interactive AL manipulator programming environment is a large step ahead of previous systems in helping users to write and debug their manipulator programs, there is still much that needs to be done. Some has already been mentioned in the previous section where various problems with the current system were discussed and possible solutions indicated. This section will point out some other areas for future work, ranging from fairly small steps to currently unbridgeable chasms.

The first step, of course, is to finish the current implementation of AL, cleaning up the various loose ends that exist. Then there are a number of extensions to the AL language—such as clauses for straight line motions, specifying the arm's configuration, or controlling new hands—which need to be added.

The large space needed to hold the parse tree for the user's program was mentioned in the previous section as a problem in that it limits the size of potential manipulator programs. Two possible routes should be investigated to allow larger programs. The simplest method is just to use a computer with a larger address space. Otherwise some or all of the parse tree will need to be compressed.

To further aid the user in teaching the positions needed when building the object models, it would be very helpful to be able to control the arm's movement with joysticks, teach boxes, speech recognizers, etc.

Much research is needed to develop better syntax-directed editors. It should be possible to make them much smarter about the language that they are dealing with. It especially should be possible to have much better error handling capabilities. For example, in the AL system a misspelled keyword can invalidate an entire line. The editor should be able to catch the error as soon as it occurs, and allow the user to fix matters. Current prettyprinting routines are just beginning to allow some of the needed flexibility.

As better interactive programming environments become available, the question arises whether manipulator programming requires a special editor and programming environment or if a general-purpose one would suffice. Certainly, there are many advantages in using existing software. Ideally, programming systems similar to today's compiler-compilers will be developed that will accept a formal definition of a desired programming language and automatically generate an editor for that language. The resulting editor would interact with a general-purpose programming environment, supplemented with a number of special-purpose routines, to allow the user to run and debug manipulator programs.

For such a general-purpose programming environment to be adaptable to manipulator programming, a number of facilities will need to be present. These primarily include support for concurrency and message passing. Special commands that would not be part of a general-purpose programming environment, such as DEFINE, AT and those for force graphing, would need to be added.

Returning to the current AL system, a graphics module needs to be added to it. There are many features above and beyond those of the old GAL subsystem that would be quite useful. These include the ability to display multiple force graphs simultaneously, and to remember collected forces across motions. Also, the user will want to view other time-related events such as position, velocity, and motor torques.

At a higher level, force sensing work needs to move beyond just using thresholds. Already several characteristic force signatures have been identified, for example, contact force; future research should uncover others. These then need to be recognized by the force system so the user can program with higher level constructs, such as "ON CONTACT DO . . . ."

As computer costs continue to plummet and the available capabilities of manipulator systems continue to increase, the number of computers in each AL-like system will grow. There are a number of problems that then arise as to how to partition the manipulator control task and how to coordinate multiple manipulators, especially when they must cooperate with each other. The type of network architecture that should be used will need to be investigated. This will get even more complicated as robotics systems move out of the laboratory and into environments where they are integrated into even larger systems.

The current AL design avails itself of the fact that there is only one interpreter and that all active processes are halted when it passes control back to the editor. In future systems this need not be the case as each manipulator may have a dedicated processor which could run its own interpreter.

The next generation of AL will need to deal with both this increased distribution of control, and the need to integrate it with larger systems. The current design does not address the issue of facilitating this integration by providing some interface to connect to these other systems, be they simple low-level vision systems, or higher level planning systems. Future systems will need to be more robust and capable of dealing with the many errors that more naive users will generate. Part of this increased robustness is facilities to calibrate the system automatically, along with tools to diagnose hardware problems with the manipulators.

Moving beyond AL, research in developing higher levels of manipulator primitives needs to be done. Such a system will need to have built-in knowledge about the manipulator's world, including geometric models of the manipulators, the objects being assembled, and the workspace. A knowledge of assembly will also be needed. At a simple level this will allow such a system to automatically derive grasp information so it can convert an object-oriented task description to one involving the manipulator. More planning knowledge will be necessary to automatically specify appropriate trajectories or to create an assembly strategy involving force sensing. While individual systems exist which are beginning to approach the level needed, they each only deal with a small part of the problem. It will still be a number of years before a complete manipulator planning system can be developed. As research proceeds, however, the capabilities of manipulator programming systems will increase and the burden of the manipulator programmer will be lightened.

Appendix A

Summary of the AL Language

A.1 Arithmetic Operations

```
scalar     s:    s+s, s-s, s*s, s/s, s↑s, |v|, |r|, |s|, v.v,
                 s MAX s, s MIN s, s MOD s, s DIV s,
vector     v:    VECTOR(s,s,s), s*v, v*s, v/s, v+v, v-v, v*v, r*v, t*v,
                 f*v, v WRT f, UNIT(v), POS(f), AXIS(r)
rot        r:    ROT(v,s), r*r, ORIENT(f)
frame      f:    FRAME(r,v), f+v, f-v, f*t, CONSTRUCT(v,v,v)
trans      t:    TRANS(r,v), f->f, t*t, INV(t)
boolean    b:    NOT b, b AND b, b OR b, b EQV b, b XOR b,
                 s < s, s <= s, s = s, s <> s, s > s, s >= s
dimension  d:    d*d, d/d, INV(d)
```

A.2 Functions

```
s:         INT(s), SQRT(s), SIN(s), COS(s), TAN(s), ASIN(s), ACOS(s),
           ATAN2(s,s), LOG(s), EXP(s), INSCALAR, RUNTIME, RUNTIME(s)
b:         QUERY(<exp>,<exp>,...,<exp>)
```

A.3 Predeclared Constants and Variables

```
s:           PI, BHAND, YHAND, GHAND, RHAND, DRIVER_TURNS
v:           XHAT, YHAT, ZHAT, NILVECT
r:           NILROT
f:           STATION, BPARK, YPARK, GPARK, RPARK,
             BARM, YARM, GARM, RARM, DRIVER_GRASP, DRIVER_TIP
             # (valid only in MOVE)
t:           NILTRANS
b:           TRUE, FALSE
strings:     CRLF, NULL
units:       CM, INCH, INCHES, OUNCES, OZ, GM, LBS, SEC, SECONDS,
             DEG, DEGREES, RADIANS, RPM
dimensions:  DISTANCE, TIME, FORCE, ANGLE, TORQUE,
             ANGULAR_VELOCITY, VELOCITY, DIMENSIONLESS
```

A.4 Statements

```
blocks:      BEGIN S; S; S; ... S END
             COBEGIN S; S; S; ... S COEND
```

```
declarations:   TIME SCALAR ts1, ts2;
                DISTANCE VECTOR dv1,dv2;
                ROT r1,r2;
                FRAME f1,f2;
                TRANS t1,t2;
                FRAME ARRAY f1[s1:s2],f2[s3:s4,s5:s6,...];
                EVENT e1,e2;
                STRING st1,st2;
                LABEL l1,l2;


procedures:     PROCEDURE p1; S;
                SCALAR PROCEDURE sp1(VALUE SCALAR vs1,vs2;
                                     REFERENCE ROT rr1;
                                     SCALAR ARRAY as1[2:3]); S;


comment:        COMMENT <any text without semicolon>;
                { <any text> }
                (* <any text> *)


control:        FOR s ← s STEP s UNTIL s DO <statement>;
                IF <condition> THEN <statement> ELSE <statement>;
                IF <condition> THEN <statement>;
                WHILE <condition> DO <statement>;
                DO <statement> UNTIL <condition>;
                CASE <scalar> OF BEGIN S;S;... S END;
                CASE <scalar> OF
                  BEGIN [i1] S; [i2] S; ... ELSE S; [i3][i4] S END;
return:         RETURN;
                RETURN(<exp>);
signal:         SIGNAL e1;
wait:           WAIT e1;


assignment:     <var> ← <expression>;


affix:          AFFIX f1 TO f2 AT t1 RIGIDLY;
                AFFIX f3 TO f4 BY t2 NONRIGIDLY;
                AFFIX f3 TO f4 BY t2 AT t1 NONRIGIDLY;
unfix:          UNFIX f5 FROM f6;


condition monitor:      (note: <rel> is ">=" or "<" )
                ON FORCE(v) <rel> <force scalar> DO S;
                ON TORQUE <rel> <torque scalar> ABOUT v DO S;
                ON |FORCE| <rel> <force scalar>
                                ALONG <axis vect> OF f1 DO S;
                ON TORQUE <rel> <torque scalar>
                                ABOUT <axis vect> OF f1 IN HAND DO S;
                ON DURATION >= <time scalar> DO S;
                ON ARRIVAL DO S;
                ON DEPARTING DO S;
                ON ERROR = s DO S;
                <label>: DEFER ON e DO S;
```

```
enable:         ENABLE <label>;
disable:        DISABLE <label>;


motion:         MOVE f1 TO f2;
                MOVE f1 TO f2 VIA f3,f4,f5;
                MOVE f1 TO f2
                        VIA f3 WHERE DURATION = <time scalar>,
                                    VELOCITY = <velocity vector>
                              THEN S
                        <more clauses>;
                OPEN  <hand> TO <distance scalar>;
                CLOSE <hand> TO <distance scalar>;
                CENTER <arm>;
                OPERATE <device> <clauses>
                STOP <device>;
                RETRY;


with clauses:   FORCE, TORQUE, DURATION  similar to condition monitor
                WITH FORCE_FRAME = f IN <co-ord sys>
                WITH SPEED_FACTOR = s
                WITH APPROACH = <distance scalar> or <distance vector>
                                   or f
                WITH DEPARTURE = <same as APPROACH>
                WITH WOBBLE = s
                WITH NULLING or NO_NULLING
                WITH FORCE_WRIST ZEROED or NOT ZEROED
                WITH STIFFNESS = (v,v) ABOUT f
                WITH STIFFNESS = (s,s,s,s,s,s) ABOUT f IN WORLD
                WITH GATHER = (FX,FY,FZ,MX,MY,MZ,T1,T2,T3,T4,T5,T6,TBL)


print:          PRINT(<exp>,<exp>,...,<exp>);
abort:          ABORT(<exp>,<exp>,...,<exp>);
prompt:         PROMPT(<exp>,<exp>,...,<exp>);
pause:          PAUSE <time scalar>;


wrist:          WRIST(fv,tv);
                SETBASE;


require:        REQUIRE SOURCE_FILE "FILE.EXT";


macro:          DEFINE <macro_name> = \ <macro_body> \;
                DEFINE <macro_name>(m1,m2,...) = \ <macro_body> \;
```

A.5 Predefined Macros

```
DIRECTLY        WITH APPROACH = NILDEPROACH
                WITH DEPARTURE = NILDEPROACH
CAUTIOUS        SPEED_FACTOR + 6.0
SLOW            SPEED_FACTOR + 4.0
QUICK           SPEED_FACTOR + 1.0
```

```
CAUTIOUSLY        WITH SPEED_FACTOR = 6.0
SLOWLY            WITH SPEED_FACTOR = 4.0
NORMALLY          WITH SPEED_FACTOR = 2.0
QUICKLY           WITH SPEED_FACTOR = 1.0
PRECISELY         WITH NULLING
APPROXIMATELY     WITH NO_NULLING
TIL               STEP 1 UNTIL
```

Appendix B

List of Commands for the AL System

This appendix lists all of the commands available in the interactive AL system. Commands are grouped according to function, that is, editor commands, debugger commands, and line editor commands.

B.1 Special Symbols

In this documentation

⟨cr⟩ is used to mean the return key,
⟨bs⟩ the backspace or delete key,
⟨space⟩ is the space bar,
⟨tab⟩ is the tab key,
⟨ff⟩ the formfeed character (SAIL only)
⟨vt⟩ the vertical tab character (SAIL only)

A prefix of "↑" is used to indicate an ASCII control character (octal 0 thru 37). Thus "↑A" means to type an "A" with the control key depressed. Note that some standard ASCII characters are in this range, so for example ⟨tab⟩ is the same as ↑I, ⟨bs⟩ as ↑H, ⟨cr⟩ as ↑M, etc. In the SAIL version certain extra control characters are available. These are denoted by ⟨cntl⟩ and are unavailable on standard ASCII keyboards, but are provided for compatibility with other SAIL utilities (line editor and E).

Certain other meta syntactic objects are enclosed in "⟨ ⟩," for example, "⟨filename⟩."

B.2 Editor Commands

Control Characters

↑A   attach (not implemented)
↑B   roll screen up to show 4 more lines at bottom

↑C	copy (not implemented)
↑D	delete *n* statements, clauses
↑E	exit
↑F	find (not implemented)
↑G	go to mark
↑I	insert line (statement, clause, label) (same as ⟨tab⟩)
↑L	go to top or line specified (e.g. ↑\22↑L)
↑N	move down (up) *n* statements (staying at current level)
↑O	move to last (= old) line
↑P	put cursor line at top/bottom of screen
↑S	move down (up) *n* statements (descending into block structure)
↑T	roll screen down to show 4 more lines at top
↑U	move up one screenful
↑V	redraw screen
↑W	move down one screenful

unused: ↑J ↑K ↑Q ↑R ↑X ↑Y ↑Z

Non-Control Commands

↑	move up to parent statement
<	move cursor down 4 lines
>	move cursor up 4 lines
⟨cr⟩	move cursor down 1 line
⟨bs⟩	move cursor up 1 line
⟨space⟩	modify line
⟨tab⟩	insert line (statement, clause, label) (same as ↑I)
\	numeric arg follows for use with command
@	move cursor to PC of current active process
[	surround a statement with a BEGIN-END block
?	help (not implemented)

SAIL only:

⟨cntl⟩⟨ff⟩	move down one screenful (same as ↑W)
⟨cntl⟩⟨vt⟩	move up one screenful (same as ↑U)

Extended Editor Commands

GET ⟨filename⟩	read in program from specified file
SAVE ⟨filename⟩	write program out to specified file
MARK	place a mark at current statement (use ↑G to move to marks)

UNMARK {ALL}   removes any mark at current statement

SET BOTSIZE #   set page printer size to #

B.3 Debugger Commands

⟨expression⟩	evaluate expression in current context and print it out
⟨statement⟩	immediately execute the statement in the current context
START or RUN	start program execution from beginning
GO	continue execution from cursor location
PROCEED	continue execution from last breakpoint
EXECUTE	execute statement pointed to by cursor
STEP	single step—descending into procedure/function calls
SSTEP	single step—treat procedure/function calls as atomic
NSTEP	single step—but stay at same lexical level
GSTEP	giant step up to level of parent statement
TSTEP	set a temporary breakpoint at current location and proceed
BREAK	set a breakpoint at cursor location
UNBREAK {ALL}	clear any breakpoint at cursor location (all breakpoints)
DEFINE ⟨varlist⟩	insert assignment statements for each variable in list
AT	update AT phrase of affixment statement
TRACE {ALL}	trace current (or all) process(es)
POP	flush outermost interpreter level
SET WAIT ON/OFF SET NOWAIT ON/OFF	turn single thread mode off/on
SET COLLECT ON/OFF	if on, then statements typed in for immediate execution will be automatically inserted into the program

Abbreviated Debugger Commands

!   debugger command follows
    !R = start   (run program)
    !P = proceed
    !S = step
    !A = sstep
    !N = nstep
    !G = gstep
    !T = tstep
    !B = break   if arg > 0, unbreak if arg < 0, and unbreak all
                            if arg = 0

B.4   Line Editor Commands

↑A	move ahead (right) one char
↑B	skip left to char next typed
↑D	delete char
↑E	skip to end of expression/line
↑F	skip to front of expression/line
↑H ⟨bs⟩	move back (left) one char (deletes last char if in insert mode)
↑I ⟨tab⟩	enter insert mode
↑K ⟨vt⟩	kill right to char next typed
↑L ⟨ff⟩	kill left to char next typed
↑M ⟨cr⟩	move cursor down one line
↑N	move cursor to next line and open it for modification
↑O	restore old line
↑P	move cursor to previous line and open it for modification
↑R	repeat last search/kill command
↑S	skip right to char next typed
↑T	transpose last two chars
↑U	move cursor up one line
↑Z	zero the expression/line
↑\	numeric arg follows for use with command

unused characters: ↑@, ↑C, ↑G, ↑J (= ⟨lf⟩), ↑Q, ↑V, ↑W, ↑X, ↑Y

SAIL only:

⟨cntl⟩⟨tab⟩	skip to end of expression/line (same as ↑E)
⟨cntl⟩⟨ff⟩	skip to front of expression/line (same as ↑F)
⟨cntl⟩⟨space⟩	move ahead (right) one char (same as ↑A)
⟨cntl⟩⟨bs⟩	move back (left) one char (like ↑H, but never deletes)
⟨cntl⟩⟨digit⟩	numeric argument for following command

Notes

Chapter 2

1. Of course, the precision of computer-represented numbers varies with the number of bits used. For typical computers, however, precision is greater than is necessary to control manipulators which are currently accurate to only a few thousandths of an inch.

2. The manipulator's position can be described in two fashions. The first describes it in real space, with three coordinates indicating the position of the manipulator's hand, and another three coordinates specifying its orientation. The second method places the position in joint space, with one coordinate for each joint, which indicates the position of that joint.

3. The AL runtime system will then do the necessary bookkeeping to maintain the correct values for the positions of these features as the object is moved about.

4. Current teach boxes consist of a number of buttons, switches, dials, and joysticks through which the user can directly control the manipulator.

5. There are often several possible ways that a manipulator's joints may be configured to reach a given position in its workspace. For an anthropomorphic, six-joint manipulator, such as the Unimation PUMA, most points in the workspace can be reached with one of eight possible arm configurations; the arm can have its elbow above or below the hand, the first-three joints can be configured to resemble a human's right or left shoulder, and the final-three joints can position the wrist in two ways. A specific position in the workspace may not be reachable with a given arm configuration since the joints have a limited range of motion.

6. In a language like AL the position recorded would be in the coordinate system of the fixed object, so if it were shifted, the mating position would also be moved appropriately.

7. The desired behavior is what the arm servo is trying to accomplish.

Chapter 3

1. In the current system if there are several expressions on the same line, as would be the case with a FOR statement, the minimal number of keywords are included in the phrase open for modification. Ideally no keywords would ever be modifiable.

2. The Stanford AL system controls three arms which are named red, green, and blue.

3. "World coordinates" refers to a fixed coordinate system in which the manipulators are calibrated.

4. This should be done with some care as the current system does not do all the checking it should. In particular jumping into the middle of a procedure or FOR loop will not always work.

5. Cartesian straight line motion has since been implemented.

6. Primarily used by people doing research in arm servo control.

7. A simple filtering scheme is used by the arm servo whereby the force must exceed the threshold for three samples before it will trigger the condition monitor.

8. Actually it was very difficult to induce the stem to jam. To do so involved tilting the sprinkler body as the arm was trying to insert the stem. Even then it still usually managed to succeed.

9. The same screen may also be used for both purposes if there is no alternative, e.g. an inexpensive computer system with only one display terminal.

Chapter 4

1. On SAIL the break character is an <escape>I.

2. The last is used by the interpreter's minimal line editor.

3. Operations such as attaching and copying statements or clauses are an obvious combination of inserting and deleting. Since they are not yet implemented no more will be said about them.

4. This has since been done; the system now uses only the incremental parser.

5. If the first token of the macro is another macro, or a parameter of one of the macros currently being expanded, then it in turn will be expanded. This process continues until a non-expandable token is encountered.

6. This is a test of pointer equivalency; no string comparisons are necessary.

7. Actually the system could ask the user just before inserting the declaration statement what type the variable should be, but this is not currently done.

8. Actually, WITH clauses require two tokens to be read.

9. For a compound statement, such as FOR, this includes initially setting the FOR body to an "empty" statement, which can later be filled in by the user.

10. Except for processes forked by a coblock which are flushed when the corresponding statement is deleted. Condition monitors are also flushed.

11. To the best of my knowledge the only recursive program actually written in AL was one I wrote to solve the towers of Hanoi problem. Since arms are not recursive devices, it is hard to think of another problem where recursive procedures would be the natural solution.

12. Any processes associated with condition monitors declared in the body of the main program are also retained.

Bibliography

[Alberga et al. 1979]
  C.N. Alberga, A.L. Brown, G.B. Leeman, Jr., M. Mikelsons, and M.N. Wegman, *A Program Development Tool*, in *Eighth Annual ACM Symposium on Principles of Programming Languages*, January 1981.

[Ambler, Popplestone, and Kemph 1982]
  A. P. Ambler, R. J. Popplestone, and K. G. Kemph, *An Experiment in the Offline Programming of Robots*, Research Paper 170, Edinburgh University A. I. Department, 1982.

[Archer, Conway, Shore, and Silver 1980]
  James Archer, Jr., Richard Conway, Andrew Shore, and Leonard Silver, *The CORE User Interface*, TR 80-437, Department of Computer Science, Cornell University, September 1980.

[Archer and Conway 1981]
  James Archer, Jr. and Richard Conway, *COPE: A Cooperative Programming Environment*, TR 81-459, Department of Computer Science, Cornell University, June 1981.

[Archer and Conway 1981]
  James Archer, Jr. and Richard Conway, *Display Condensation of Program Text*, TR 81-463, Department of Computer Science, Cornell University, 1981.

[Archer 1981]
  James Archer, Jr., *The Design and Implementation of a Cooperative Program Development Environment*, TR 81-468, Department of Computer Science, Cornell University, 1981.

[Barstow, Shrobe, and Sandewall 1984]
  David R. Barstow, Howard E. Shrobe, and Erik Sandewall, editors, *Interactive Programming Environments*, McGraw Hill, 1984.

[Berez 1978]
  Joel M. Berez, *A Dynamic Debugging System for MDL*, TM-94, Laboratory for Computer Science, M.I.T., January 1978.

[Binford et al. 1975]
  T. O. Binford et al., *Exploratory Study of Computer Integrated Assembly Systems*, Progress Report No. 2, Stanford University, 1975.

[Binford et al. 1976]
  T. O. Binford et al., *Exploratory Study of Computer Integrated Assembly Systems*, Progress Report No. 3, STAN-CS-76-568 (AIM-285), Stanford University, August 1976.

[Binford et al. 1977]
  T. O. Binford et al., *Exploratory Study of Computer Integrated Assembly Systems*, Progress Report No. 4, AIM-285.4, Stanford University, June 1977.

[Blume 1981]
  Christian Blume, *A Structured Way of Implementing the High Level Programming Language AL on a Mini- and Microcomputer Configuration*, in *Proceedings of the 11th International Symposium on Industrial Robots*, October 1981.

[Bolles and Paul 1973]
Robert C. Bolles and Richard Paul, *The Use of Sensory Feedback in a Programmable Assembly System*, STAN-CS-73-396 (AIM-220), Stanford University, October 1973.

[Burkhart and Nievergelt 1980]
H. Burkhart and J. Nievergelt, *Structure-Oriented Editors*, Swiss Federal Institute of Technology, May 1980.

[Buxton and Stenning 1980]
J. N. Buxton and V. Stenning, *Requirements for Ada Programming Support Environments—'Stoneman'*, U.S. Department of Defense, February 1980.

[Chu et al. 1982]
Yaohan Chu, Kozo Itano, Yasushi Fukunaga, and Marc Abrams, *Interactive Direct Execution Programming and Testing*, TR-1149, Maryland University Computer Science Center, 1982.

[Craig 1985]
John J. Craig, *Introduction to Robotics: Mechanics and Control*, Addison Wesley, 1985.

[Danthine and Geradin 1984]
Andre Danthine and Michel Geradin, *Advanced Software in Robotics*, North-Holland Publishing Company, 1984.

[Darringer and Blasgen 1975]
John A. Darringer and Michael W. Blasgen, *MAPLE: A High Level Language for Research in Mechanical Assembly*, IBM Research Report RC-5606, September 1975.

[Donzeau-Gouge et al. 1975]
V. Donzeau-Gouge, G. Huet, G. Kahn, B. Lang and J.J. Levy, *A Structure-oriented Program Editor: A First Step Towards Computer Assisted Programming*, in *International Computing Symposium 1975*, North-Holland Publishing Company, 1975.

[Finkel et al. 1974]
Raphael Finkel, Russell Taylor, Robert Bolles, Richard Paul, and Jerome Feldman, *AL, A Programming System for Automation*, STAN-CS-74-456 (AIM-177), Stanford University, November 1974.

[Finkel 1976]
Raphael A. Finkel, *Constructing and Debugging Manipulator Programs*, STAN-CS-76-567 (AIM-284), Stanford University, August 1976.

[Geschke 1978]
Clifford Calvin Geschke, *A System for Programming and Controlling Sensor-Based Robot Manipulators*, UILU-ENG-78-2230, University of Illinois, Urbana-Champaign, December 1978.

[Gini and Gini 1983]
M. Gini and P. Gini, *From Goals to Manipulator Programs*, TR 83-514, Department of Computer Science, Minnesota University, 1983.

[Goldman and Mujtaba 1981]
Ron Goldman and Shahid Mujtaba, *AL User's Manual*, Third Edition, STAN-CS-81-889 (AIM-344), Stanford University, December 1981.

[Good 1981]
Michael Good, *Etude and the Folklore of User Interface Design*, ACM SIGPLAN Notices, Vol. 16, No. 6, June 1981.

[Grossman and Taylor 1975]
David D. Grossman and Russell H. Taylor, *Interactive Generation of Object Models with a Manipulator*, STAN-CS-75-536 (AIM-274), Stanford University, December 1975.

[Grossman 1977]
David D. Grossman, *Programming a Computer Controlled Manipulator by Guiding Through the Motions*, IBM Research Report RC-6393, March 1977.

[Habermann 1979]
A. Nico Habermann, *An Overview of the GANDALF Project*, in *CMU Computer Science Research Review 1978–79*, Carnegie-Mellon University, 1979.

[Halbert 1978]

Daniel C. Halbert, *A LISP Debugger for Display Terminals*, M.I.T., May 1978.

[Horton 1981]

Mark R. Horton, *Design of a Multi-language Editor with Static Error Detection Capabilities*, UCB/ERL M81/53, Electronics Research Laboratory, U.C. Berkeley, July 1981.

[Hünke 1981]

H. Hünke, editor, *Software Engineering Environments*, North-Holland Publishing Company, 1981.

[IEEE 1983]

IEEE Conference on Software Development Tools, Techniques, and Alternatives, IEEE Computer Society Press, 1983.

[IEEE 1983]

IEEE Workshop on Languages for Automation, IEEE Computer Society Press, 1983.

[Inoue et al. 1981]

H. Inoue, T. Ogasawara, O. Shiroshita, and O. Naito, *Design and Implementation of High Level Robot Language*, in *Proceedings of the 11th International Symposium on Industrial Robots*, October 1981.

[Ivie 1977]

Evan L. Ivie, *The Programmer's Workbench—a Machine for Software Development*, *Communications of the ACM*, Vol. 20, No. 10, October 1977.

[Kanasaki, Yamaguchi, and Kunii 1982]

Katsumi Kanasaki, Kazunori Yamaguchi, and Tosiyasu Kunii, *A Software Development System Supported by a Database of Structures and Operations*, TR 82-15, Department of Information Science, Tokyo University, 1982.

[Koutson 1981]

A. Koutson, *A Survey of Model Based Robot Programming Languages*, Working Paper 108, Edinburgh University A.I. Department, 1981.

[Knuth 1983]

Donald E. Knuth, *Literate Programming*, STAN-CS-83-981, Stanford University, 1983.

[Lacos and McDermott 1982]

C. A. Lacos and T. S. McDermott, *Interfacing with the User of a Syntax Directed Editor*, R82-3, Department of Information Science, University of Tasmania, 1982.

[Latombe and Mazer 1981]

Jean-Claude Latombe and Emmanuel Mazer, *LM: A High-level Programming Language for Controlling Assembly Robots* in *Proceedings of the 11th International Symposium on Industrial Robots*, October 1981.

[Lieberman and Wesley 1977]

L. I. Lieberman and M. A. Wesley, *AUTOPASS: An Automatic Programming System for Computer Controlled Mechanical Assembly*, *IBM Journal of Research and Development*, Vol. 21, No. 4, July 1977.

[Lozano-Pérez 1976]

Tomás Lozano-Pérez, *The Design of a Mechanical Assembly System*, AI-TR-397, M.I.T., December 1976.

[Lozano-Pérez 1982]

Tomás Lozano-Pérez, *Robot Programming*, AI-TR-698, M.I.T., 1982.

[Mason 1982]

Mathew T. Mason, *Manipulator Grasping and Pushing Operations*, AI-TR-690, M.I.T., 1982.

[Medina-Mora and Feiler 1981]

Raul Medina-Mora and Peter H. Feiler, *An Incremental Programming Environment*, *IEEE Transactions on Software Engineering*, Vol. SE-7, No. 5, September 1981.

[Medina-Mora 1982]

Raul Medina-Mora, *Syntax-Directed Editing: Towards Integrated Programming Environments*, Department of Computer Science, Carnegie-Mellon University, 1982.

[Meyer 1981]

Jeanine Meyer, *An Emulation System for Programmable Sensory Robots*, IBM *Journal of Research and Development*, Vol. 25, No. 6, November 1981.

[Mikelsons and Wegman 1980]

M. Mikelsons and M.N. Wegman, *PDEIL: The PL1L Program Development Environment, Principles of Operation*, IBM Research Report RC-8513, October 1980.

[Mikelsons 1981]

Martin Mikelsons, *Prettyprinting in an Interactive Programming Environment*, ACM *SIGPLAN Notices*, Vol. 16, No. 6, June 1981.

[Morris and Schwartz 1981]

Joseph M. Morris and Mayer D. Schwartz, *The Design of a Language-Directed Editor of Block-Structured Languages*, ACM *SIGPLAN Notices*, Vol. 16, No. 6, June 1981.

[Mujtaba 1982]

Mohamed Shahid Mujtaba, *Motion Sequencing of Manipulators*, STAN-CS-82-917, Stanford University, July 1982.

[Nevatia and Binford 1973]

R. Nevatia and T.O. Binford, *Structural Description of Complex Objects*, in *Proceedings of the Third International Conference on Artificial Intelligence*, Stanford University, August 1973.

[Park and Burnett 1979]

William T. Park and David J. Burnett, *An Interactive Incremental Compiler for more Productive Programming of Computer-Controlled Industrial Robots and Flexible Automation Systems*, in *Proceedings of the 9th International Symposium on Industrial Robots*, 1979.

[Paul 1973]

Richard P. Paul, *ARM.LOU[UP,DOC]*, internal documentation, Stanford Artificial Intelligence Laboratory, October 1973.

[Paul 1976]

Richard P. Paul, *WAVE: A Model-Based Language for Manipulator Control*, The *Industrial Robot*, Vol. 4, No. 1, 1977.

[Popplestone, Ambler, and Bellos 1978]

R. J. Popplestone, A. P. Ambler, and I. Bellos, *RAPT: A Language for Describing Assemblies*, The *Industrial Robot*, Vol. 5, No. 3, September 1978.

[Reps 1981]

Thomas Reps, *Optimal-time Increment Semantic Analysis for Syntax-directed Editors*, TR 81-453, Department of Computer Science, Cornell University, March 1981 (revised November 1981).

[Reps 1981]

Thomas Reps, *The Synthesizer Editor Generator: Reference Manual*, Department of Computer Science, Cornell University, September 1981.

[Reps 1982]

Thomas Reps, *Generating Language Based Environments*, TR 82-514, Department of Computer Science, Cornell University, 1982.

[Rich and Shrobe 1978]

Charles Rich and Howard E. Shrobe, *Initial Report on a LISP Programmer's Apprentice*, IEEE *Transactions on Software Engineering*, Vol. SE-4, November 1978.

[Rosen et al. 1977]

C. Rosen et al., *Machine Intelligence Research Applied to Industrial Automation*, Seventh Report, SRI International, August 1977.

[Salisbury and Craig 1981]

J. Kenneth Salisbury and John J. Craig, *Articulated Hands: Force Control and Kinematic Issues*, *International Journal of Robotics Research*, Vol. 1, No. 1, Spring 1982.

[Salisbury 1982]
J. Kenneth Salisbury, Jr., *Kinematic and Force Analysis of Articulated Hands*, STAN-CS-82-921, Stanford University, July 1982.

[Samuel 1980]
Arthur Samuel, *Essential E*, STAN-CS-80-796 (AIM-335), Stanford University, March 1980.

[Sandewall 1978]
Erik Sandewall, *Programming in an Interactive Environment: the "LISP" Experience, ACM Computing Surveys*, Vol. 10, No. 1, March 1978.

[Satterthwaite 1975]
Edwin Satterthwaite, Jr., *Source Language Debugging Tools*, STAN-CS-75-494, Stanford University, May 1975.

[Shapiro, Collins, Johnson, and Ruttenberg 1980]
E. Shapiro, G. Collins, L. Johnson, and J. Ruttenberg, *PASES: A Programming Environment for Pascal*, Yale University, April 1980.

[Shimano et al. 1984]
Bruce E. Shimano, Clifford C. Geschke, Charles H. Spalding III, and Paul G. Smith, *A Robot Programming System Incorporating Real-Time Supervisory Control: VAL-II*, in *Proceedings of the Robots 8 Conference*, Society of Manufacturing Engineers, June 1984.

[Soroka 1980]
Barry I. Soroka, *Debugging Robot Programs with a Simulator*, presented at CADCAM-8 Conference, Society of Manufacturing Engineers, November 1980.

[Summers and Grossman 1981]
Phillip D. Summers and David D. Grossman, *XPROBE: An Experimental System for Programming Robots by Example*, IBM Research Report RC-9082, October 1981.

[Swinehart 1974]
Daniel C. Swinehart, *Copilot: A Multiple Process Approach to Interactive Programming Systems*, STAN-CS-74-412 (AIM-230), Stanford University, July 1974.

[Takase, Paul, and Berg 1979]
Kunikatsu Takase, Richard P. Paul, and E.J. Berg, *A Structured Approach to Robot Programming and Teaching*, in *Proceedings COMPSAC 1979*, November 1979.

[Taylor 1976]
Russell Highsmith Taylor, *A Synthesis of Manipulator Control Programs From Task-Level Specifications*, STAN-CS-76-560 (AIM-282), Stanford University, July 1976.

[Taylor, Summers, and Meyer 1982]
R. H. Taylor, P. D. Summers, and J. M. Meyer, *AML: A Manufacturing Language*, IBM Research Report RC-9389, April 1982.

[Taylor 1983]
R. H. Taylor, *An Integrated Robot System Architecture*, IBM Research Report RC-9824, 1983.

[Teitelman 1977]
Warren Teitelman, *A Display Oriented Programmer's Assistant*, CSL 77-3, XEROX Palo Alto Research Center, March 1977.

[Teitelbaum 1981]
Tim Teitelbaum, *The Cornell Program Synthesizer: A Tutorial Introduction*, Department of Computer Science, Cornell University, August 1980 (revised January 1981).

[Teitelbaum and Reps 1981]
Tim Teitelbaum and Thomas Reps, *The Cornell Program Synthesizer: A Syntax-directed Programming Environment*, Department of Computer Science, Cornell University, 1981.

[Teitelbaum, Reps, and Horwitz 1981]
Tim Teitelbaum, Thomas Reps, and Susan Horwitz, *The Why and Wherefore of the Cornell Program Synthesizer, ACM SIGPLAN Notices*, Vol. 16, No. 6, June 1981.

[Unimation 1979]
Unimation, Inc., *User's Guide to VAL, A Robot Programming and Control System,* Unimation, Inc., Version 11, February 1979.

[Van Harmelen 1983]
F. A. H. Van Harmelen, *On the Implementation of an Editor for the B Programming Language,* Mathematisch Centrum, Amsterdam, 1983.

[Verhelst and Verster 1981]
P. W. E. Verhelst and N. F. Verster, *PEP: an Interactive Programming System with an Algol-like Programming Language,* Mathematisch Centrum, Amsterdam, August 1981.

[Wilander 1979]
Jerker Wilander, *An Interactive Programming System for Pascal,* Informatics Laboratory, Linköping University, Sweden, November 1979.

[Wilcox, Davis, and Tindall 1976]
T. R. Wilcox, A. M. Davis, and M. H. Tindall, *The Design and Implementation of a Table Driven, Interactive Diagnostic Programming System, Communications of the ACM,* Vol. 19, No. 11, November 1976.

[Will and Grossman 1975]
Peter Will and David Grossman, *An Experimental System for Computer Controlled Mechanical Assembly, IEEE Transactions on Computers,* Vol. C-24, 1975.

[Wood 1981]
Steven R. Wood, *Z—The 95% Program Editor, ACM SIGPLAN Notices,* Vol. 16, No. 6, June 1981.

[Zellweger 1983]
Polle T. Zellweger, *An Interactive High Level Debugger for Control Flow Optimized Programs,* CSL 83-1, XEROX Palo Alto Research Center, 1983.

[Zellweger 1984]
Polle T. Zellweger, *Interactive Source-Level Debugging for Optimized Programs,* CSL 84-5, XEROX Palo Alto Research Center, May 1984.

Index